DATE DUE			
Oct 27 '76			
Jul 6 '77			
Aug 12 '80			
Feb 8 '81			
Mar 13 '81			
2/18/81 10:00			
Apr 20 82			
APR 10 1987			

JULIE HARRIS

TALKS TO YOUNG ACTORS

JULIE HARRIS

TALKS TO YOUNG ACTORS

By JULIE HARRIS with
BARRY TARSHIS

Lothrop, Lee & Shepard Company · New York

TO YOUNG ACTORS

CONTENTS

PREFACE

Most of the material in this book was gathered from lengthy tape-recorded conversations at Julie Harris' home in Westchester County, New York, during the summer of 1970. We would meet on the average of two or three times a week, depending on her schedule, and at each session we tried to concentrate on one particular aspect of acting life.

After a session, I would arrange and shape Julie's comments into a rough draft, which she would look over and revise, and which I then took back a second time and, in some cases, a third and fourth time, until we had struck the exact chord.

As a writer, I benefited immeasurably from this collaboration. This was not merely because it enabled me to meet and get to know a remarkable actress and a unique, warm, thoughtful, and enchanting woman, but because so much of what Julie Harris has to say about acting can just as easily be applied to writing or, for that matter, to any art form, particularly in the uncompromising attitude toward honesty.

Certain acknowledgments are in order: to Joan Rubin, the editor of *Playbill* and a dear friend, who originally asked me to do the magazine profile that first introduced me to Julie and indirectly led to the book; Joan Korman, who was my agent at the time the idea for this book was conceived; Lynn Paulsen, Linda Feick, Christine Cammarano, and Nancy Murray, who helped us with research; theatrical agent Fifi Oscard, who provided information about breaking into the theater today; and Harry Mastergeorge, of the American Academy of Dramatic Arts, who helped bring Julie together with a large group of young acting students and thus proved that Julie's approach to life and to acting is extremely relevant to young people today; and, of course, to my wife, Karen.

BARRY TARSHIS

How calmly does the orange branch
Observe the sky begin to blanche
Without a cry, without a prayer,
With no betrayal of despair.

      · · · · ·

Oh Courage, could you not as well
Select a second place to dwell,
Not only in that golden tree
But in the frightened heart of me?

TENNESSEE WILLIAMS,
The Night of the Iguana

·1·

WHY IS AN ACTOR?

You say to yourself, I want to get out, I'm going to get out, and when I get out of this, I will show them, I will show them, I will show them, without having the faintest idea of how you're going to show them. I simply had this driving ambition—I was going to be a simply smashing actor.

—LAURENCE OLIVIER, from an
interview with theater critic Kenneth Tynan

"Things happen," the novelist D. H. Lawrence wrote, "and we have no choice."

It's difficult for me to pinpoint exactly what in my life led me into acting. As it is with so many actors, it wasn't just one thing, but a combination of things.

Throughout most of my childhood and adolescence, I was the classic wallflower: skinny, awkward, self-conscious about my teeth braces, shy with boys, quarrel-some with my parents. Even school was a struggle for me. It was all I could do to simply pass my subjects.

There were a few things I could do well. One of them was to mimic people. Another was to do little improvisations that made people laugh. My brother and I, I remember, liked to act out together scenes from movies we'd been taken to see.

Of course, most children are good at this sort of playacting, for making believe comes close to being an instinct. So it never occurred to me as a little girl, as much as I was fascinated by the movies and by the stage, that I could take this small talent that I had and build a life around it.

My parents were an important influence. Neither of them had ever been in show business professionally, but both were devoted to the arts, particularly music and theater. My mother was forever telling me about the plays she saw and loved so much when she was in her early twenties and working as a nurse in New York City.

My father headed his dramatic group in high school, and although the main avocation in his life after college

was mammology, a branch of zoology, I wonder sometimes if he wasn't sorry he hadn't followed up on his
acting. He often reminded me that I was not the first
member of the family to act in New York. When he
was a freshman at Yale, he had played Agamemnon in a
spoof of Euripides' *Iphigenia in Aulis*. The production
had a Christmas vacation run in New York at a place
called The Little Theatre.

My parents introduced my two brothers and me to
the theater early in life. We lived in Grosse Pointe,
Michigan, a suburb of Detroit, and I can't remember a
time when I wasn't going with my mother to a children's theater or the ballet or the movies.

I was ten when I first began going with my parents to
the Cass Theater in Detroit. This, to me, was the ultimate in sophistication—to actually see in person some
of the famous actors I'd seen in movies or had heard my
parents talk about. Over the next few years I would see
Helen Hayes, the Lunts, Katharine Cornell, Maurice
Evans, Ethel Waters, and Al Jolson, and they would
make an impression upon me that I would never forget. Even today, I can picture, clear as day, and even
hear in my mind, Ethel Waters singing "Taking a
Chance on Love" in *Cabin in the Sky*.

If there was a turning point in my life, it came during
my freshman year of high school. About that time, a
young woman who had just graduated from Vassar College came to our school to teach drama. Her name was

Betty Spencer, and she was filled with wonderful ideas. One of the first things I did for her was to play the lead in a stage version of the French story *The Juggler of Notre Dame*. I don't remember much about the role itself, only that when the show was over, many people—not just my mother and father—made it a point to tell me how good they thought I was.

This was a new experience. I was frequently told that I was too thin, that I wasn't doing well enough in Latin and algebra, and that I was sometimes difficult to get along with. But, until that evening, nobody had ever gone out of his way to tell me that I was actually *good* at something.

It overwhelmed me. It was as if, after all those years, I'd discovered a secret power. I wasn't sure exactly what this power was, but I certainly wasn't going to let it get away from me.

So the only things that really meant anything to me in high school, the only things I really cared about, were drama classes and after-school drama activities. I didn't want to waste time shopping for clothes. I refused to "come out." I didn't worry that I was not doing very well in my other classes. Acting was all that mattered.

My parents at this point were mildly encouraging. They thought it was a stage I was going through and didn't try to influence me one way or the other. They agreed to let me go to a theater camp at Steamboat Springs, Colorado, for three summers. There I took acting courses with Charlotte Perry and dance courses with Valerie Bettis. What a marvelous experience! It was Miss Perry, really, who persuaded me to pursue acting as a career. Her encouragement led me to apply after high school to the Yale Drama School. At that time—the end of World War II—Yale was accepting people who were not college graduates. It was during the year I spent at Yale that I auditioned for—and got my first part in—an actual Broadway play. The play was called *It's a Gift*. It ran for only six weeks. When it was over I went back to Yale to finish out the term. I was only nineteen at the time and it would be another five years before I would become an "overnight success" in *The Member of the Wedding*. But "success" was not the most important thing then. Suddenly I was in the business. I was an actress. There was nothing else I wanted to do, little else I was qualified to do. Things had happened, and I had not had a choice.

If you're in your teens, you might well feel as I did when I was your age. You want to act. You want to be an actor. Something inside tells you, you have something to contribute, something to express. Perhaps nobody but you takes these ambitions very seriously. Your parents would like to see you work harder in school. Your friends think you're crazy. If you're lucky, there are one or two people—the drama teacher at school perhaps—giving you encouragement.

In this book I am neither going to discourage you

from going into acting nor am I going to paint a false and rosy picture. I am going to try to tell you what I think about acting, about the theater, about films, and what acting has meant to me personally. I do this knowing that what I have to say may not agree with what you think or with what other people have said or written. And I do this knowing that my background might be quite different from yours, so that what worked for me is not necessarily going to work for you.

[Acting, after all, is very personal. You can theorize all you want, but in the final counting, it all comes down to how and what you communicate to your audience. When you're onstage and performing, the audience doesn't care where you were born, where you went to school, how many acting lessons you've taken, how well you slept the night before, or what you had for breakfast that morning. The concern is, simply, are you getting to them? Are they interested in and moved by what you're doing? That's all that matters.]

Some of the marvelous performances I've seen in my life, Laurette Taylor in *The Glass Menagerie*, Ethel Waters in *The Member of the Wedding*, Lee J. Cobb in *Death of a Salesman*, and Laurence Olivier in *Oedipus*, all prove this point. Each time it was as though the actor were saying something to me personally, revealing to me something about the human condition that I hadn't been aware of before. It's what Helen Hayes calls "the moment of miracle," when the actor and the audience get together. When this happens, acting becomes much more than a craft. It becomes a true art.

They say of Edwin Booth, whom many consider the greatest tragedian ever to act upon the English-speaking stage, that acting was his way of communicating to his audience something that was central to his nature: his love of the beautiful. Booth lived only for his art. Each time he performed he was sharing his own view of life, his particular vision, with the audience.

Too often, when acting is discussed, this concept of "giving" and "communicating" is overlooked. But I know myself—and I think I can speak for many actors—that I do my best work when I am filled with a sense of mission toward the audience, when I am involved with something that they *must* be made aware of.

Nothing thrills me more as an actress than to give recitations of Emily Dickinson's poetry. Her poetry has meant much to me personally, and I want to share this feeling with others. A simple line: "The heart asks pleasure first,/And then, excuse from pain." It isn't enough simply to recite this line. I want to go into the audience, to say the line to each person individually.

In every actor you'll find something of the missionary —the feeling that he must get his message across to *everybody*. Actors are often accused of being exhibitionists. Yet few actors act for themselves alone. We act out not only our own fantasies but the fantasies of the people who come to see us. "You're the daughter I never had," a woman who had seen me in *East of Eden* wrote me years ago.

And here, really, is why success—real success—is so elusive to the actor, why the threat of failure haunts nearly everything we do. If someone has invested time and money to watch me, and if he isn't impressed or moved by what he has seen, then I have failed him. And if I fail him, I fail myself.

Let me give you an example: In 1960, I opened on Broadway in a play called *Little Moon of Alban*. It had originally been produced on television and in it I played an Irish Sister of Charity, Brigid Mary. I can think of no other part, with the exception perhaps of Joan of Arc in Jean Anouilh's *The Lark*, that I felt more deeply and intensely. Opening night I gave what I thought was a good and honest performance. The audience seemed moved; they believed me, and most of the critics liked what I did. Except one man, one reviewer. My performance, he said, didn't go "deep enough."

Not deep enough! What did he mean, not deep enough? If this characterization, one I felt more deeply than almost anything I'd ever played, wasn't deep enough, then clearly it meant that I was a failure as an actress. And if I was a failure as an actress, what had I been doing with my life for the past fifteen years.

Someone else might have burned that review, or sent it back to the writer. I didn't. I pasted it up on my dressing-room mirror and each time I looked at it tears came into my eyes. It was a week before I took it down, a month before I could think about it without getting upset. I recovered, of course. We all do. But the worst part is, if the same thing were to happen today, if someone were to come up to me after a performance to tell me that I didn't "feel" the part enough, I'd probably react the same way.

I admit it. I am addicted to my work, my craft. I can honestly say that no role in my career has come easy. I work as hard today on a new role as I did when I first began acting. But even so, I think it's worth the effort—well worth the effort. For sometimes acting *can* be the perfect experience—when you are able to do your job perfectly and the audience receives it, and gives some understanding back to you. Then there is real communication.

In my lifetime it has happened a few times—a performance in which everything—all the costumes, the props, the words, and the true and universal emotion communicated itself to the audience through me. I recall one night in particular; it was during the run of *The Lark* on Broadway in 1955. In the scene in which the Earl of Warwick comes to visit Joan in prison after she has recanted, something happened. I'd done the part many times, in rehearsals and in performances. But on this particular evening when I started to speak the lines, I couldn't because I was crying. Part of me was trying to pull me out of this emotion so I could speak my line. Another part was saying that what was happening was right for the part, right for this particular moment. Yes, for this is probably what Joan would have done. And the audience knew it and was thrilled by it. For me, it was an almost spiritual experience.

Months later when we were in Los Angeles, in the road company of *The Lark*, again something just seemed to click in a performance, not just with me but with all of us; and when it was over the audience continued to applaud long after we'd gone back to our dressing rooms to change—that's how moved they were.

It is tempting, of course, to over-romanticize the work of an actor. The fact remains that acting is mostly work and sweat. Much of what we do is routine and workaday. There is plenty of drudgery and frustration, too. For some people, acting is simply a job—a way to make a living, a skill, like cabinetmaking. They scoff at the idea that there is any real self-expression or art in what we do.

I think an actor who develops this attitude automatically limits himself. For acting *can* be an art. It all depends upon what the actor is willing to contribute to it. Arthur Miller described in a *Holiday* magazine article a supreme moment in the theater that occurred during a rehearsal of his play *Death of a Salesman*. Lee J. Cobb, who had been struggling with the part up to then, stood up and said to Mildred Dunnock, who played his wife, "I was driving along, you understand? ... And then all of a sudden I'm goin' off the road! ..."

"And the theatre vanished," Miller wrote. "The stage vanished. The chill of an age-old recognition shuddered my spine; a voice was sounding in the dimly lit air up front, a created spirit, an incarnation, a God-like creation was taking place; a new human being was being formed before all of our eyes, born for the first time on this earth, made ready by an act of will by an artist's summoning up of all his memories and his intelligence; a birth was taking place above the meaningless traffic below; a man was here transcending the limits of his body and his own history."

Miller went on: "When I hear people scoffing at actors as mere exhibitionists, when I hear them ask why there must be a theatre if it cannot support itself as any business must, when I myself grow sick and weary of the endless waste and the many travesties of the most abused of all arts, I think of Lee Cobb making that role and I know that the theatre can yet be one of the chief glories of mankind."

·2·

BORN TO ACT

A tremendous amount of preparatory work and continuous training is necessary to turn your vague wish into professional excellence, so that in the end you are not a wunderkind, or a talented dilettante, but a true actor, a master of your craft.

—ALEXANDER TAIROV, *Notes of a Director*

Everybody is a born actor. What child doesn't like to dress up and play grown-up? And what grown-up doesn't tell a lie from time to time or pretend to be angry with a child when he's not or act politely in front of someone he'd really like to punch in the nose?

Naturally this doesn't mean that anyone on the street can stop whatever he's doing and play Hamlet. But it does mean that everybody has the basic capacity, a potential, which if developed can perhaps produce an accomplished actor.

Thomas Wolfe wrote in his novel *The Web and the Rock*: "If a man has a talent and cannot use it, he has failed. If he has a talent and uses only half of it, he has partly failed. If he has a talent and learns somehow to use the whole of it, he has gloriously succeeded, and won a satisfaction and a triumph few men ever know."

This statement applies to acting in the following way: The poor actor is not necessarily the one who lacks raw talent—voice, looks, imagination, and so forth. He is usually the actor who has never learned to use or has not been motivated to use the "whole of it."

I don't deny the importance of certain native-born gifts. But regardless of what you've been blessed with at birth, nothing will materialize unless your potential is mobilized and channeled into one direction. Talent, in other words, is always subordinate to the uses to which it's put.

And talent is not an absolute—a fixed entity that resists change and growth. Talent can—and must—be developed. The key is motivation.

In acting there is simply no substitute for motivation. Lee Strasberg, the director and co-founder of the Actors Studio, used to constantly compare the acting process with the long, arduous process of becoming a concert violinist.

I agree with what he said. And I say the only way you can possibly go through this long and arduous process of becoming an actor is to *want* it or *need* it badly to begin with. There is no way to overstate the amount of hard work, tedium, frustration, and disappointment that fills the career of an actor. If you're not strongly motivated, you simply won't put up with it. Instead of going to bed early the night before an important audition, you'll go out with friends. Instead of working on your part at home, you'll watch television. And as the pressure of an opening night begins to build and you haven't really mastered your part, you'll ask yourself, "Why do I need this?" and you may quit.

So there can be no escaping the demands. If you want to become a successful actor, you must accept the fact that the development process is infinite. The good actor is always striving, always learning, always improving, long after he has established himself. Great actors get better with age. Olivier works with more intensity and concentration today than twenty-five years ago. Sarah Bernhardt was as active in her sixties as she was in her twenties. "You're never too old to play St. Joan,"

Dame Sybil Thorndike once told another actress, Zoe Caldwell. "You're only too young."

Few people outside the theater can even begin to appreciate the amount of work and time it takes to develop into a true actor. Not a personality. Not a type. Not a person who repeats himself with every characterization. But a master of your craft. And by master of your craft, I mean the master of a technique that you can count on night after night in any and all situations.

In Japan an actor who joins the all-male Kabuki is prepared to spend five years of rigorous study before he has thoroughly mastered the motions and sounds needed to make him believable as a woman. Actors in China study for nine years before they consider themselves professional enough to perform in front of an audience. The French actor François Talma always insisted an actor needed twenty years to master his profession.

Not many American actors have this sort of patience. In America the emphasis is usually not on artistic development but on career success. Richard Chamberlain, the young actor who was a success as Dr. Kildare on television, left Hollywood to join a provincial repertory theater in England. It ultimately led to his performance as Hamlet on network television. Some people may not have agreed with his Hamlet, but that isn't the point. The point is that Richard cared enough about his craft to go where he could develop it.

The greatest single problem facing the young American actor today is that he doesn't have much chance to grow as an artist. The artistic climate in the United States doesn't foster gradual, long-range development. The number of repertory theaters in the United States is increasing, but we still have nothing in this country to compare with the Abbey Theatre of Dublin or the Old Vic or the Royal Shakespeare Company or Olivier's National Theatre in London.

One of the luckiest things to happen in my career was to be taken in as a walk-on one spring when the Old Vic Theatre came to Broadway. The company at that time included Ralph Richardson, Laurence Olivier, Joyce Redman and Margaret Leighton. I had never seen ensemble acting like this before. It was like hearing a symphony orchestra. Each night the notes were struck the same way, with the same intensity and simplicity. Yet the performance always seemed to live for the first time, as if it had never happened before.

Just watching these people act night after night for six weeks was a revelation. It inspired me to work that much harder on my own acting. It proved to me that an actor could develop a well-trained instrument, that he could be a consummate craftsman, but could still be extraordinarily fresh and creative. And moving.

Call it osmosis, or what you will, but when you are

actually working with or watching actors like Olivier and Richardson, it cannot help but teach you and inspire you. I really hope that someday this country will be able to offer the young actor a training experience similar to those available in certain European and Asian countries, particularly England, France, and Russia: a place to learn all the aspects of theater art: music, singing, diction, dance, costume and scene designing, training in the classics, and the opportunity to work with a first-class repertory company, playing walk-ons, then small parts, and gradually building toward playing leading roles—always surrounded by the example of gifted actors.

So, in the absence of this kind of environment, the American actor must meet the problem of artistic growth pretty much on his own. It isn't easy, but I think there is much that can be done.

There is no reason, for instance, that a young actor should consider himself exempt from the preparatory work that young people in the fields of music and athletics take for granted. Is there a concert pianist alive who hasn't spent years practicing scales and other exercises to develop a masterful technique? Is there a tennis champion who didn't start learning the game before he was ten, spending years just perfecting the basics? Is there a successful artist who hasn't used up hundreds of sketchbooks?

Most of the preparatory work for an actor needn't

cost much. It doesn't even require a teacher or a coach. You can begin by going to a library and taking out the biographies of famous actors of the past. Read about David Garrick, Henry Irving, Ellen Terry, Eleonora Duse, Edwin Booth, the Barrymores. See what made them unique. See what they did in order to achieve greatness.

Read plays. The great plays of Shakespeare, Euripides, Chekhov, Shaw, O'Neill, O'Casey, Ibsen. Director Tyrone Guthrie referred to these works as "dramatic cathedrals." "Their implicit meanings," he said, "are like echoes in a cathedral." Read them aloud. Get the feel of what great drama is.

Get in the habit of memorizing. Start out with poetry you like. Or psalms. Then go into some of the Shakespearean soliloquies and sonnets. Learn an entire role. Never mind that you have no ambition to ever play Shakespeare. I say, read the plays and familiarize yourself with the parts anyway. The work will benefit you no matter what roles you go into later. And you never know. In five years you may want very much to be a Shakespearean actor.

In every great actor there is a sense of always seeking something beyond himself. It's what the Russian director Konstantin Stanislavski would have referred to as "pursuing a higher degree of excellence." W. C. Fields is a perfect example. He began as a juggler. But he didn't want to be *just* a juggler. So he began using lines in his act. And then he began incorporating situations into the act. He was always adding something. He never stopped growing.

Whatever skills you learn now in your youth will help you somehow in your acting. I think of Christopher Plummer, who studied piano as a boy. We did Ibsen's A *Doll's House* together on television. When the time came for Torvald Helmer to play a tarantella, Chris did it himself.

Language skills can be extremely valuable. I've worked on parts in which I've had to speak French. In *I Am a Camera* I had many lines in German. In *Anastasia* I had some Russian to speak. These linguistic problems caused me enough difficulty to make me wish I'd applied myself a little more in high school.

Read. Learn. Absorb. Give yourself fully to life. "Learn about people," Helen Hayes said in an interview in the book *Actors Talk about Acting*. "Not just the people you encounter, but what people of all ages, of all times have written. Craftsmanship is not enough. An actor must enrich his life by studying literature, science, philosophy, other countries, other peoples, other times."

I love what Olivier once told critic Kenneth Tynan: "You've got to find in an actor a man who will not be too proud to scavenge the tiniest little bit of human circumstance; observe it, find it, use it some time or another."

If I were starting out now, I would begin keeping a notebook, the way many writers do. In it I would make notes of people I'd seen on the street who looked interesting, of how people walk and sit, of mannerism and speech characteristics.

The time to begin all this is *now*, while you're young, while you're still in school, while you have the time to learn and explore and discover. The faculties you have been born with, the potential you have, the desire— none of it will take you very far unless you seize these things and direct them toward a goal. Don't delay. Before you know it, time will have slipped by, and as an actor—and a person—you will be all the poorer.

·3·

THE SOLDIER'S
DISCIPLINE

It had been drilled into us that when an audience pays to see a performance, it is entitled to the best perform-ance you can give. Nothing in your personal life must interfere, neither fatigue, illness, nor anxiety—not even joy.
—LILLIAN GISH, *The Movies, Mr. Griffith and Me*

"Those civilians," June Havoc likes to say, referring to anybody who isn't involved in the theater, "they just don't know what it's like."

Probably the most difficult thing for a "civilian" to

grasp about acting is the monumental amount of work —physical and mental work—involved with the craft. I still meet people who think the hardest thing about acting is memorizing lines. Actually, learning lines is one of the simpler aspects of acting.

As an example, let's say you're playing a role in a typical television series. An average working day is twelve hours.

If you're on location, you work in all sorts of weather. I've worked full days when the temperature was 104 degrees in the shade, days when my skin turned so red I had to stop working two or three times to take a cold shower.

And acting has its occupational hazards, too. As long as I live, I'll never forget the day I was stepped on by a full-grown lion. It happened while I was working as a guest star on the *Tarzan* television series. In the script, I was supposed to be lying unconscious, and a lion was supposed to come up to me, sniff, and then go away. It was a trained lion, of course, and he'd been de-clawed. To make him walk up to me, the director put a platter of milk near my shoulder. The lion came into the scene on cue, but nobody told him he wasn't sup-posed to stand on the actress's chest. Imagine lying on your back with your eyes closed, feeling pressure on your chest, looking up, and then seeing a lion. I jumped with a muffled scream and ran off the set, and I was very lucky I didn't panic the lion, Ralphie.

But the pressures are more than just physical. In recent years the theater, television, the film industry—all of it has become more cost and time conscious than ever before. Production costs have risen enormously, so everything must be compressed into as short a time period as possible.

An average hour-long program for a television series is shot in nine days. The entire production schedule, down to the last detail, is mapped out ahead of time. Every facet of the schedule is coordinated.

For the actor, there is little room for deviation. Whether you are "inspired" on a particular day is immaterial. You are expected to show up on time, in command of your lines, and in peak physical shape. You never say to a movie director, "I don't think I can do this today. Can we do it tomorrow?"

The rules are strict and unyielding. No actor, regardless of his stature, is exempt from them for very long. Few personalities are so important that they can't be replaced if they don't meet the demands. Actors who don't meet the demands ultimately find it difficult to get work.

Among the big names of Hollywood—Richard Burton, Elizabeth Taylor, John Wayne, Marlon Brando, Paul Newman, Joanne Woodward, Audrey Hepburn, Katharine Hepburn, and others—discipline is second nature. They approach their work as professionally and in as businesslike a manner as a doctor or lawyer or banker. The same was true of such actors as Clark Gable, Humphrey Bogart, Gary Cooper, and Spencer Tracy. It didn't matter where they'd been or what they had done the night before. When the time came to start work in the morning, they were waiting and ready.

Certain actors, on the other hand, have magnificent potential but never develop the discipline needed to survive. The most tragic example is Marilyn Monroe.

Here was a wonderful actress and a sensitive and loving woman whose life and career were cut short. Why? Because she couldn't find it in herself to meet the everyday demands of the profession, such as following directors' orders or coming to the set on time.

Had Marilyn been as disciplined an actress as Lillian Gish, I think she would be alive today. It seems to me that the people around her whom she trusted should have been prodding her to systematize her life in order to make the most of her talent. Instead, they indulged her lack of discipline.

Discipline. I have a simple definition of it: doing what is required of you regardless of your problems and fears. And with discipline comes courage—the courage to extend yourself, to subdue with your own resources your personal demons. Discipline and courage. No great actor has been without them.

·4·

THE ACTING MACHINE

. . . it's a very hard life. The hours are different from the rest of normal living, and in order to be able to act well, you have to be in marvelous physical condition.
—VIVIEN LEIGH, *Actors Talk about Acting*

With few exceptions, sickly people do not become successful actors. Marcel Proust may have written his greatest works while bedridden. And Paul Gauguin could still paint in his final years even though he couldn't walk. But for the actor, the stage is the only battlefield. You have to be *there*, burning with will and energy.

Probably the most exhausting show I ever worked in was *Marathon '33* with June Havoc. Even before rehearsals started for that play, I worked for six weeks with Timmy Everett on the difficult jazz dances needed for the marathon scene. We went over and over the same steps until I could see them in my sleep. Rehearsals began, and a week later I needed a shot of B-12 just to keep me on my feet one day so I could drag my partner Lee Allen around on the dance floor. Eventually I grew stronger. By the end of rehearsals, I was strong enough to lift a chair with one hand.

Another time, in the musical *Skyscraper*, we were in a pre-Broadway run in Detroit when the producers and director decided the show needed a rewrite. We had to learn—I should say relearn—almost half the script in a day and a half, from Sunday to the performance Monday night, and that included new lines with old cues, old lines with new cues, and new lyrics. We made it— with sheer will and strong coffee and a prayer to St. Jude.

Fortunately, I have been blessed with pretty good stamina. I might be a little too high strung for my own welfare, but I have always enjoyed good health. I've worked at it. I eat sensibly. I try to sleep at least eight hours a night, more if I'm working. If I feel myself getting run-down I take vitamin pills. I'm an ardent believer in exercise. When I was younger I swam and played tennis. Nowadays I get most of my exercise by working around the house and by walking. I love to walk!

But health is such an individual matter. Sarah Bernhardt, for instance, rarely went to bed earlier than 4 A.M. and rarely got up later than 7 or 8 A.M. But Madame Sarah didn't smoke, and she took catnaps throughout the day. I, too, love to nap. A short nap—ten or fifteen minutes in my dressing room, on a table, a bench, or even the floor—can give me an enormous lift.

Still, I can't keep late hours the way Sarah Bernhardt did; nor do I know many actors who can. The body, after all, is only a machine. "Thine evermore, most dear lady, whilst this machine is to him," Hamlet writes to Ophelia. And if we misuse this machine, we will wake up one day and find out it no longer responds.

Diet is so important! I've heard that the Comédie Française insists that each of its students take a course in basic nutrition. What you eat affects your energy, your resistance, even your frame of mind. Eating the wrong kinds of food can spoil your complexion. Avoid too many starches and fried foods, sweets and carbonated drinks. If you drink coffee, do it in moderation. Eat foods rich in protein: meat and fish and fresh leafy vegetables. Keep fresh fruit on hand. Instead of candy, eat an apple. And if you're working in a show, eat as if you were a marathon runner.

As far as smoking is concerned, I can do no better

than to echo Agnes De Mille's advice to young dancers. "Do not learn to smoke." I started smoking in high school and wish I hadn't. It has always given me coughing problems. It complicates matters whenever I catch a cold. I've been waging a constant battle with smoking for as long as I can remember, trying my hardest to give it up. But you become a slave to it. I've managed to cut down some, but it still plagues me. My advice from personal experience: Don't start.

Exercise, as I said earlier, is essential. Running, tennis, swimming, gymnastics—anything is good that tones up your muscles and improves your wind. Many actors lift weights. Dance exercise classes are marvelous for young actors. Ballet lessons—anything that puts you in touch with your body is helpful.

Finally, we come to the question of drugs. I've yet to hear a convincing argument as to why *actors* should take them—I know many reasons why they shouldn't.

The first and most obvious reason—apart from health —is that in order to act well, you must be able to concentrate. And to concentrate you have to be in complete control of your body, your mind, and your emotions. The moment you release some portion of that control to an outside agent, a drug, you're compromising yourself as a performer.

Secondly, the unpredictability of many drugs affects not only *your* performance, but also the cohesiveness of a whole group of actors. I once worked in a play in which an actor came to the theater "high" on several occasions. His eyes would be glazed and he always seemed on the verge of falling over. He didn't really react onstage, and it affected everyone's timing. Ultimately, he was asked to leave the cast.

Drinking presents the same problems. An actor who drinks is usually unpredictable to work with. I remember one performance in which an actor was so drunk we had to hold him up and whisper his lines to him. It was one of the most horrifying nights I ever had in the theater.

I've heard some actors say they work better when they're under the influence of some drug such as marijuana. I don't believe it. They may *think* they're acting better, but I refuse to believe that pills or drugs of any sort will make a person a better actor. Too many great actors have gotten along without them. Good actors don't need to get "high" for a performance any more than good athletes need to get "high" for an important game.

A far more serious problem than marijuana, to my mind, is the increased reliance among theater people on pep pills and barbiturates. Because of the long hours and the many pressures, many actors learn to depend on pills such as Benzedrine or Dexedrine. Some reach a point where they need as many as seventy a day.

If you're hooked on pep pills, you also need barbiturates at night to help you fall asleep. And the longer you rely on barbiturates, the more you have to take if they are to be effective.

Pill addiction is probably as bad as alcoholism. Think of the great entertainers we have lost through barbiturate overdoses.

I will go to any length to avoid taking pills. There have been periods in my life when I simply had to take some medication in order to sleep, but the few experiences I've had with sleeping pills have left me feeling more tired and groggy than before.

But how do you deal with fatigue? And how do you deal with insomnia? I say, with discipline. The best way to combat fatigue is to avoid it—that is, to be in such peak physical condition that your endurance is never overtaxed. Sometimes, of course, you're extended beyond your normal powers. And here's where strength of mind is important. You *force* yourself to stay in command of the situation. You *force* yourself to stay alert and to concentrate.

Insomnia. It's been a problem since the beginning of time. And everybody has to work it out in his own way. I find that a glass of milk or a glass of stout before bed helps me to relax. If I see I'm having trouble relaxing, I open my eyes, concentrate on some object in the room, and then take some very deep breaths.

Sometimes it works. If it doesn't, I occasionally go over in my mind a long part I know from start to finish. If I'm lucky, I'll be asleep midway through the first act.

I know of some actors who have learned to hypnotize themselves to sleep and others who've been helped through Yoga exercises. Just about anything is better than sleeping pills.

Remember also that the effect of one or two sleepless nights isn't as damaging as you might think and doesn't necessarily mean the pattern will continue. If you can't sleep, don't lie in bed brooding about it. Get up. Take a walk. Read. Do laundry. Do *something*.

To repeat, I feel very strongly about drugs. I don't believe that anyone needs them in order to act. As far as getting "turned on," I can only say this: I wish for you that your work will "turn you on," that the excitement and the thrill and the responsibility of acting in a production will sustain you and that you will not need an artificial method of finding the meaning of things.

·5·

THE TOOLS OF ACTING

The actor brings to his art an instrument already created—himself.
— LEE STRASBERG, *Strasberg at the Actors Studio*

Acting, like any craft, requires certain tools—things you use to do your job. The actor's job is to make the audience believe he is another human being and to do this in a meaningful and moving way. How does he do this? By means of certain tools, such as his voice, appearance, and body movement. These are to the actor what paints, canvas, and brushes are to the painter. Anyone can go out and buy the basic tools of painting. Not everybody can paint. Everyone has a voice and an appearance. Not everyone can get onstage and create illusion.

But the acting instrument consists of other tools, too. Internal tools: imagination, sensitivity, intelligence. Every good actor, in one way or another, relies on these internal tools as much as the external tools. The better the actor, the more he makes use of *all* his tools, internal and external.

Many misconceptions surround the acting instrument—that combination of physical gifts and mental attributes needed to produce an accomplished actor. Take appearance. Many people, particularly young people, believe that in order to become a successful actor, you have to *look* a certain way. "I want to be an actor," a young person will say, "but I don't think I'm handsome enough."

This is a foolish attitude. If you are blessed with natural beauty or good looks, it can be of tremendous help in your career, no doubt about it. But most of the great actors throughout history—and most of the actors who work regularly today—are not really beautiful or handsome in the way these terms are usually understood. You may think you're too short or too tall or that your nose is too big or not big enough, your hair too straight or too curly. But none of these things need impede your career. Sarah Bernhardt was described by Cornelia Otis Skinner as having the body of a "consumptive wraith," and with hair that was a "reddish blonde mop, thick, fuzzy and completely unruly." Edwin Booth was a small, slight man—inconspicuous from a distance, but with magnificent eyes.

And that's the point. There may be *one* thing about you that's arresting. And that's the thing you should build on. None of the great English actors of our time —Laurence Olivier, John Gielgud, Ralph Richardson, and Sir Michael Redgrave—has the near perfect good looks of the male models in advertisements. And many very successful American actors have exploded the myth that in order to *be* a movie star you have to *look* like one.

What you need is not natural beauty or good looks. You need a strong sense of personal style—something that separates you from everybody else. Take Zero Mostel, for example. He is not a handsome man. He has a huge body, a comic face. He's nearly bald. Yet he has a wonderful sense of style, a genuine flair, and a positively hypnotizing stage presence. He wasn't born with this; he developed it. The fact that he is also a painter probably taught him the marvelous variety of effects he can achieve through very subtle changes in his appearance— by moving a tuft of hair from one side of his forehead to the other, for example.

Barbra Streisand! I think she's a fantastically beautiful woman. She's all style. Everything about her—the way she dresses and wears her hair—it all has a wonderful continuity. There's only one Barbra Streisand and only one Garbo, just as there was only one Gary Cooper and one Humphrey Bogart.

You, too, are *one*. There's no one like you in the world. As the Gentleman Caller tells Laura in Tennessee Williams' *The Glass Menagerie*, you are "one times one." What you have to do is figure out which personal style best suits *you*. You have to *think* about yourself and study yourself. Find out which colors suit you best. Experiment to see which hair length and style best projects *you*. You can do it today more than ever before, because there has never been as much freedom of expression in clothes and makeup and hairstyles.

When Edith Piaf entertained, she rejected the traditional nightclub dress, and wore, instead, just a simple black dress with a heart-shaped neckline. The dress was designed by Coco Chanel, and with Chanel simplicity. And the dress *was* Edith Piaf, and no one else. There are countless other examples: Charlie Chaplin, W. C. Fields, Mae West. In every instance, the key was not just the way they looked, but the image they projected. Each projected a definite identity. Each dressed and acted in concert with that identity.

As for voice, the same thing holds true. Too many young actors worry unnecessarily about the *sound* of their voice, whether it's high or low or guttural. They seem to think that there is such a thing as an "acting voice" and that to be an actor, you have to modify your own speaking instrument to make a particular sound. I say, don't worry so much about the *sound* of your voice. Be conscious instead of the *meaning* of what you're saying. And don't be in too much of a hurry to seek the help of a voice coach. It's liable to do you more harm than good.

The one great voice teacher I've known (and I am not talking about a singing coach) was the late Iris Warren, who worked with me at Stratford, Canada. She recognized that every actor had different vocal needs. She treated each actor individually and applied no set rules. "There is no such thing as an acting voice," she used to say. "Every actor has to find his own way of conveying meaning."

This isn't to say you should ignore your voice entirely. A voice must have power enough to project. It must be flexible enough to convey a broad spectrum of emotional colors, especially for Shakespeare and any verse part. I learned to project and to color my voice by doing it onstage. But if I were starting fresh, I would most certainly take singing lessons. Singing lessons teach breath control. And provide the kind of vocal flexibility an actor needs. Even if you don't take singing lessons, sing anyway, sing on your own, in the school glee club, in a church choir.

But again, a warning. Don't put all your emphasis on the sound of your voice. I know of some actors whose voices are so rich and mellow and so cello-like that I get shivers listening to them. But then if I concentrate, I begin to sense that the voice alone is doing most of the work. Sound overwhelms meaning. The voice is acting on its own. It's not connected to the feelings.

Good diction, of course, is important. You must be understood onstage! I've had a lot of drill; lessons have taught me that when I speak, I must dot every *i* and cross every *t*. I guess if I hadn't gone through the process of trying to speak correctly, I would be that much poorer in my speech patterns. But the important thing, in taking diction lessons, is to see this not as an end but as a means. Speech must always be the servant of the emotions. If you can't feel what you're speaking, you're not doing your job.

Perhaps you speak with a regional dialect or an ethnic accent. Should you work to get rid of it? No law says you should. Charles Boyer never did. Neither did Walter Slezak. But by keeping your accent or drawl, you limit the number of roles you can play.

Shedding your accent isn't as difficult as you may think. Murray Hamilton worked systematically to lose his southern drawl, but it came in handy when he played the rich Southerner in *The Hustler*. And Sidney Poitier had a very strong West Indian accent when he began acting, but lost it by listening to words and phrases on the radio and then repeating them aloud.

An actor must be able to move well with grace and

sureness. To be sure of yourself onstage, you must be able to move with agility. But bear in mind that, even if you aren't especially well coordinated or agile, you can develop these qualities through training and practice. You can improve your sense of balance, for example, by doing a simple exercise. Stand for as long as you can on one foot with your eyes closed. Then the other foot. You should be able to stand that way for at least ten seconds, providing there is nothing physiologically wrong with your equilibrium. On your own, you should practice sitting down and getting up, training yourself not to miss the chair or get entangled in your clothing.

The whole point of this training is to make your body—every part of your body—instantly responsive to what you have to do onstage. You should be so sure of your movements onstage that you don't have to think about them. You're not worried about pouring water from a pitcher. Or lighting a cigarette or a candle. Or running offstage. Whenever the legendary actress Eleonora Duse had a long crossover to make, she would first count the number of steps it took her to get from one side of the stage to the other, then she practiced this movement with *her eyes closed*. She did it again and again until it became second nature to her.

"I'm good," Marlon Brando once said, "when I forget." I think what he meant was this: When he wasn't worried about his lines or whether his voice would carry or anything that he had to do technically onstage, he could concentrate on being truthful to the dramatic situation.

So also, with the basic acting tools. You master them through training, practice, and hard work, but when the time comes to go to work onstage, you forget about them. You know that whatever you call on them to do, they will be responsive.

·6·

IMPACT
THE ULTIMATE TOOL

The secret of great acting, I suppose, is that some-where inside the actor something happens that just hits the audience so hard.
   —JOSÉ FERRER, *Actors Talk about Acting*

Emily Dickinson once said that she could tell she was reading a truly great poem if it made her feel as if her head were coming off. I feel the same way about great acting performances. Something happens between the actor onstage and me, sitting there in the audience. It's the communication I talked about earlier—the sense that whatever the actor is going through at this moment, I have gone through, too. We are sharing a moment together, the actor and I, as if the two of us were alone and revealing to one another our most heavily guarded secrets.

Acting, we must never forget, is an emotional craft. There is a kind of surrealism in great acting performances. No one understands it fully. Great actors are sometimes referred to as somnambulists—sleepwalkers. Why and how they do it, nobody knows—not even the actor himself. "The impact, impact, impact," José Ferrer says when he tries to explain the chemistry between the great actor and his audience. "If you are supposed to cry, [a great actor] makes you cry more deeply."

I can speak only for myself. The performances I remember are those in which a great amount of feeling was being generated onstage, layers and layers of emotion. And the performances I have given that have produced the strongest audience response were performances in which I, as an actress, was strongly and emotionally wound around what I was doing onstage.

Here is an oversimplification, but it helps to explain, I think, what we mean by impact. An aerial photograph of a flooded area doesn't have nearly the *impact* on a magazine reader as a close-up photograph of a woman weeping over her destroyed home. What moves us is not so much events in themselves, but the impact these events have on human beings with whom we can identify.

Sensitive people tend to be understanding and sympathetic. Because they respond to situations in their own life with feeling and intensity, they can understand this response in other people and in the characters that playwrights create. In some people this sensitivity is instinctive. In others, it must be first thought out and intellectualized.

"Think about what that character is feeling" is an instruction that actors hear over and over in rehearsal. Can you do it? Hamlet in a particular scene is going through a personal crisis. Do you understand what he's feeling? Can you empathize with what he's going through? Can you relate what he's going through to something that's happened in your own life? This is what we mean by sensitivity—the ability to detect in others their emotional responses to a situation and to honestly relate these responses to your own life.

Can sensitivity be taught? Is it something you are born with or not? I don't know for sure. It has more to do with the way in which your personality takes shape, I think, than with your endowment at birth. It's hard to say what makes one person more intense, more responsive, and more sensitive than someone else. It has to do, perhaps, with the experiences you have while you're growing up. "It was really life, itself, that prepared me for my acting career," Simone Signoret has said. She added: "I don't necessarily believe that the life of an actor should color his work—it is enough that he be sensitive and receptive to what goes on around him. I do believe, however, that the actor should have meaningful and personal points of reference from which he can draw."

Is it enough to be sensitive and receptive to what goes on around you? Yes! In this respect, you *can* develop sensitivity—by not closing yourself off emotionally, by being open to the infinite variety of life going on around you. You don't have to understand and appreciate Mozart in order to appreciate the absolute rapture a true Mozart lover experiences whenever he's at a concert. What is needed is your *willingness to accept the possibility that someone could be so moved.* This is what is meant by being receptive, and this willingness to accept grows, the more you yourself see and observe and experience. You can develop it through reading, through travel, through conversation. One day you meet someone who is wild about stamp collecting. And instead of saying to yourself "How could anybody in his right mind get excited about stamps?" you say, "Isn't it marvelous how excited and involved he can get over something? I can appreciate that."

But being sensitive and receptive is not enough. You still must communicate this understanding to an audience. And here is where imagination becomes important, and why pantomime practice and training are so essential to the development of an actor.

Everybody has an imagination. But not everybody

uses it to the same extent. At the Actors Studio we were often asked to impersonate inanimate objects. "Julie," Lee Strasberg would say, "be an Etruscan vase. Or be a tree." And at first I would think, How can I be a vase? How can I be a tree?

Other actors had the same thoughts because some of them gave up. But I would say to myself, "Okay, how can I be a tree?" I would picture in my mind what a tree looked like. I would concentrate on that tree. And if I concentrated long enough, it would work. And Mr. Strasberg would say to the other students, "Now look at Julie. There's a tree."

Does this mean that I had a greater imagination than the other students? Not at all. It means that I *forced* my imagination to work for me. The imagination doesn't work on its own. It must be coaxed and pushed first, then it gathers its own momentum. Think of your imagination as if it were a large wagon sitting at the top of a hill. If you want it to go down the hill, you have to first get it started. Then it will move on its own. Halfway down, it might slam against the curb. You have to pull it back and redirect it again.

This is why it's wrong for an actor to say in a special situation, "I can't do that. I can't be a tree or a vase. I can't say that line." If you begin with that attitude, you'll *never* do it. What you have to tell yourself is, "Right now, I might not be able to see myself do this particular thing, so I must work with my imagination so that I can."

Imagination is a wonderful, limitless tool. It has few boundaries. But you must not be afraid of it. The entire structure of the Stanislavski theory of acting rests on the idea that the actor has within himself, within his own imagination, a vast treasure of fully realized experiences—lifetimes and lifetimes of emotional responses. The point of Stanislavski's teaching is to explore this vast area we call the imagination, to ferret out from it those genuinely felt responses that can be used—again, the tool—onstage in a particular situation.

Let's go back a moment. We begin with sensitivity—an ability to feel, understand, empathize with someone else's experience. Next we take imagination—the force we use to take what we see, hear, and discern from others and relate and connect these things to our own experience. But there is still another step in the acting process. For lack of a better word, I call it *acting intelligence*.

Intelligence when used in the acting process has nothing to do with education or the number of books you've read or your ability to explain Einstein's theories.

Acting intelligence, as I see it, has to do with making choices. It is the one tool of acting that serves as an umbrella for all the rest. None of the other tools—voice, movement, appearance, imagination, sensitivity—can work unless it is mobilized and channeled into one specific direction. And the force that channels these tools, the force that tells us which tools to use when, this force I call acting intelligence.

Take a typical acting situation: a scene in which an actor is supposed to express rage. There are many ways an actor can get this message across to the audience, many choices. But only certain choices will work, will convince and involve the audience, within the context of this particular dramatic situation. Intelligence consists of knowing what will work at a given time. Some call it an actor's instinct. Maybe it is instinctive to a certain extent. But mainly it is something that develops throughout a career.

Children often make marvelous actors because they have not yet learned to intellectualize what they do. They feel something onstage, they express this feeling honestly and clearly, and the audience responds.

But there are times in acting when the process is not as simple and direct. No child, no matter how gifted, is going to be believable as Macbeth or Hamlet or Juliet. For that matter, many successful and basically competent adult actors couldn't begin to tackle these roles. You don't realize just how monumental the challenges of acting really are until you start preparing for a long classical role. In just one Shakespearean soliloquy, there are crescendos of emotions. To do a role like Juliet well, it's not enough to understand the character, to memorize the lines, even to speak the difficult speeches with force and clarity. A role like that demands superior voice control. You have to be able to cry, wail, scream, rant. You also need emotional control so that the next night you'll be able to repeat it again.

You possess a magnificent voice. Intelligence tells you how to *use* that voice. You make a wonderful appearance onstage. Intelligence tells you how much makeup you need to enrich that appearance. You have a ballet virtuoso's control over your body. Intelligence tells you when to slouch, how to convey emotion through simple gestures—a shrug of the shoulders, a turn of the back. You are deeply sensitive and have a rich imagination. Intelligence puts that sensitivity and imagination to work!

A painter can have all the physical tools of his craft and possess a marvelous facility, but without vision, without some highly personal statement, some strongly felt sense of truth, the work remains hollow and easy to forget.

Acting intelligence is to the actor what that sense of vision is to the painter.

·7·

AUDITIONS
HOW TO SURVIVE THEM

I had been too quick to jump to conclusions; get my feelings hurt; decide, because things hadn't gone easily for me, that they didn't want me. If I had stayed I might have made a better impression on the next reading. That taught me a lesson that I never forgot. Always stay . . . and hope, as long as there is any hope, that you can finally bring the thing off.
—KATHARINE CORNELL, *I Wanted to Be an Actress*

Auditions are a fact of acting life that every actor, one way or another, must come to grips with in his own way. Some people think the entire audition system is wrong and cruel, that a single audition doesn't really show what an actor can do. But the fact remains that the system exists, and we simply must face up to it. Long after I was an established actress, I still had to audition. In the movies, screen tests are routine for even big-name stars.

All in all, I haven't done too badly with auditions throughout my career. Actors have their strengths and weaknesses, and one of my strengths has always been the ability to pick up an unfamiliar script for the first time and give it a fairly passable first reading. I haven't always been successful, certainly. One of my big disappointments was not being chosen to replace Julie Andrews as Eliza Doolittle in *My Fair Lady*. I've had my nightmarish moments, too. When I auditioned for Eva Le Gallienne's repertory theater, which is no longer in existence, I was so nervous onstage that I had to stamp my feet first to keep my legs from shaking. The people watching must have thought I had some sort of palsy. I was not taken into the company.

Around the same time, I was invited to read for a part in John Synge's *The Playboy of the Western World*. It was only a small part, but I loved the play. I've always loved things Irish, and I wanted the part badly. The director was the late Guthrie McClintic, who was Katharine Cornell's husband—a wonderful, dear man. When I got to the office, before I even read, he told me, politely and diplomatically, that they had decided to give the part to someone who was really Irish.

If this were to happen to me today, I know what I would do. "What do you mean, really *Irish?*" I would bellow in the thickest Irish brogue you can imagine. "I'm as Irish as anybody in the world."

But in those days I didn't have more than a shred of confidence, so when this happened I just stood there a moment, dumbfounded. I tried to contain myself but tears started rolling down my cheeks. I fled from the office. Rather than wait for the elevator, I stumbled down twenty flights of stairs. I was still crying when I got to the bottom.

The odd part of this story is that Mr. McClintic called two days later to tell me he had changed his mind. I'm sure he simply felt sorry for me, and probably thought to himself, Well, it's only a small part, and who knows what this poor girl will do if she doesn't get it. But I don't recommend tears as a way of getting a role. Not many directors are as sympathetic, as gentle, or as sentimental as Guthrie McClintic.

You almost never audition for a play in the professional theater without first going through a preliminary interview with the producer or with a member of the production company. The one exception is the "open audition," held for Broadway musical tryouts. Some open auditions are held solely for members of Actors

Equity, a trade union that represents theater actors, but some are open to anyone who wants to go down and audition. Unless you know what to expect, your first open audition can be a traumatic experience. Hundreds of people show up, and the auditions are run as though you were on a factory assembly line. You may find, once you've gone out on the stage, that someone will interrupt you in the middle of a song. It can be a depressing experience, and you have to be prepared for it.

Interviews are arranged in a different way. Theoretically, every member of Actors Equity is entitled to an interview for every new part that becomes available in a new Broadway show, but this agreement is mostly a contractual obligation between the producers and Equity. The notices are usually posted on the bulletin board in the Equity office in New York, and most of the time an interview consists of dropping off some photographs and a résumé at a producer's office.

Often agents arrange interviews. An agent gets a request from a casting director for a specific type, and the agent sends actors who fit the general description.

But you don't need an agent and you don't have to belong to Actors Equity in order to get an interview. If you have the desire and the energy, you can go on your own to offices of producers who are casting plays. It's referred to as "making the rounds" and can be an enormously discouraging experience. Very often you never get by the receptionist. But if you happen to be right for a particular role, and you time your visit properly, you might be invited to audition.

Many people talk about the luck involved in getting a part—the fact that you happen to be at a certain place at a certain time. But as long as you keep from getting discouraged, you can create your own opportunities. You must believe in yourself, no matter what. Eventually, if you have the talent, you will connect.

The interview that precedes the audition is usually very short. Most of the time, it's a question of how physically right you are for the part. Personally, I wish this weren't so. Typecasting is characteristic of theater and film in America, and it works to the disadvantage of many talented actors. In any case, the impression you make at an interview is every bit as important as the impression you make at an audition. Come looking your best. Be direct, courteous, and pleasant. Don't be afraid to tell the person you're speaking to what you can do, but don't overdo it, and don't burden the interviewer with your personal problems. And be yourself.

As far as the audition itself goes, the best advice I can give is this: Whatever you do, don't be tentative. Go into the audition with a fixed idea in your mind of what you're going to do and then just do it. Try not to worry about how it will turn out.

In high school, the year we did Oscar Wilde's *The*

Importance of Being Earnest, several of us auditioned for the Lady Bracknell role. Even though I looked less like Lady Bracknell than anybody I can think of, I got the part. I got it because, when I auditioned, I read the part the way I imagined a character actress named Edna May Oliver would have read it. My reading had a focus, a life of its own. The other readings didn't.

Another instance comes to mind. A summer theater group was holding auditions one spring in a dingy office above the Belasco Theatre in New York. I did a scene from George Bernard Shaw's *Caesar and Cleopatra.* At one point in the scene Cleopatra grovels at Caesar's feet.

The floor was filthy. I imagine that some actresses might have merely simulated that portion of the scene in which Cleopatra has to flatten herself on the ground. But dirty as the floor was, I groveled on it. My dress was ready for the cleaners. And one of the producers was so appalled by what I did that he walked out of the office. But the other producers were impressed. They accepted me, and later one of them said: "We figured anybody who wanted to act *that* badly deserved a chance."

The actual conditions surrounding auditions vary considerably from place to place. There's quite a difference between auditioning for a high school play, when there may not be more than five or six of you trying for the same part, and auditioning for a Broadway production when there may be four hundred other actors also being considered.

But regardless of the circumstances, the basic problem is the same. You have to demonstrate some spark, some quality, something unique that will separate you from all the other people who are competing with you. One television casting director gives the following advice to the aspiring actor: "When casting, I look for surprise. Something fresh. I look for one actor with a completely different and fresh approach to the material used. I don't care if he fluffs 50 percent of the material just so there is something unique about his reading."

The actor's chief enemy at an audition is usually himself. There's no way that you can control the circumstances or the conditions of the audition itself, but you can control your reactions to it. Above all, you must be prepared for the unexpected. You may show up at the theater for an audition one afternoon and find an atmosphere of chaos. Actors are being crammed in a little area backstage. It's hot and uncomfortable. The stage manager is rude and edgy. Maybe there are some workmen making repairs around the stage.

You have no control over these things. To worry about them is pointless and self-defeating. To complain about them is useless. You have to somehow transcend them. You have to do your best no matter what.

One of the best ways to cope with the unpredictable is to do as much as you can to prepare yourself beforehand. Most of the time, even if it is a new play, you can find out something about the character. If you can get the script ahead of time, do it. Call the producer and ask if you can borrow the script overnight or go up to the office to read it. I am astonished at the number of actors who show up for auditions and readings and simply stumble their way through. It's plain that they haven't spent a moment at home thinking about what they're going to do onstage.

There's no excuse for coming unprepared to an audition. If you give a reading from a familiar play, you ought to know at least some speeches in the part backwards and forwards. This means you've worked on it, hours at a time, on your own.

Very often, of course, you're asked to read "cold," from a script you've never seen before. When this happens, you'll usually be given a few minutes to look the speech over, or else be told briefly what the scene is about. If you're not given time, I suggest you ask for a few minutes. Almost always you'll get it. You can accomplish much in these few moments. Don't worry so much about reciting each line correctly. Instead, try to get some idea in your mind how the scene should go. Imagine for a moment that you're an artist working on a new canvas. The first thing he does is to sketch in the broad outline. That's what you should do at a first reading.

In one respect, you can even prepare yourself for

cold readings. Get a book of unfamiliar plays and pretend you've been asked to audition for some of them. Pick scenes at random. Pick different characters. Give yourself different time limits. Use your imagination. Pretend you're alone on a Broadway stage or in front of a movie camera and that a director is hanging on every word you say.

Something else you can do to give yourself confidence is to memorize on your own as many scenes and as many different kinds of material as you can. Very often, after you've read for the director a scene that he has selected for you, he'll ask you to recite something else. And here's a wonderful opportunity to recite something that shows you at your best—something you've worked on and perfected. This doesn't happen all the time, of course, but when it does happen, you should be prepared for it.

Once you've come to an audition prepared, the next thing to do is to forget for the moment that you're auditioning and concentrate instead on being an actor. If it's a musical audition and you're expected to either dance or sing, try your hardest to enjoy the singing and dancing for their sake alone. Maybe this sounds absurd —*enjoying* an audition—but don't think of it as an audition. You're doing the sort of work you like to do. It's your talent, your life.

Brandon de Wilde was only one of hundreds of boys who read for the part of John Henry West in Carson

McCullers' *The Member of the Wedding*. But Brandon came fresh, scrubbed, and smiling. He really looked at me when I read with him. He looked at me and he "listened . . ." He had never acted or auditioned before, and I don't think he really cared one way or the other if he got the part. But he was so unaffected, so natural, so much himself, so warm and sunny—he stole everyone's heart and got the part hands down. I'm not saying you shouldn't care about getting a part, only that your anxiety over the role should never make you lose your naturalness or your sense of warmth.

I remember Paul Roebling, one of many, many actors who auditioned for the part of the Dauphin in *The Lark*. Paul came to the audition as if it were the actual performance. He'd combed his hair in an appropriate way and brought with him the stick and ball game that the Dauphin plays with throughout the scene. He created the Dauphin for us completely, and he got the part.

What I'm saying here, really, is that the audition is in itself a performance, calling for the same skills and same mental awareness you need at an actual performance. Accept the fact that you're going to be nervous. Nearly everyone is to some degree. But here's where discipline and courage assume importance. Discipline helps you to keep your wits about you regardless of how trying the circumstances are. Courage helps you walk out onstage in spite of your fear. One feeds on the other. The more discipline you impose upon yourself, the more courage you develop. The more you force yourself to act despite your fear, the less difficult it becomes the next time.

One of my favorite passages from Joan of Arc deals with this very problem.

"What do you do when you get scared?" the Dauphin Charles asks Joan.

"Act as if I wasn't," she replies. "It's that simple. Try it, say to yourself 'Yes, I am afraid. But it's nobody's business, so go on, go on.' And you do go on."

And Charles asks, "Where do you go?"

Joan answers, "To the English, outside Orléans, and when you get there and see the cannon and the archers, and you know you are outnumbered, you will say to yourself, 'All right, all right, they are stronger than I am, and that frightens me, as well it should. But I'll make myself go on because I had sense enough to get frightened first.'"

The worst mistake you can make at an audition is to get angry at the people around you, either your fellow actors or the people conducting the audition. You may have just cause. A stage manager might be sarcastic. You might be kept waiting backstage or in an office waiting room for an hour or so. But, I say, stick it out and never lose your own sense of who you are and your own sense of what's right or wrong.

If a stage manager is brusque and sarcastic with you,

it doesn't help matters to be brusque and sarcastic back. Ignore it. Remember, too, to be considerate of the other actors at the audition. We'll talk about the etiquette of acting in a later chapter. For now, it's enough to remind you that your fellow actors are going through the same sort of nervous crises that you're going through. Any little kindnesses you can do for one another will benefit everyone in the long run.

What you wear at an audition isn't as important today as it used to be, when actors dressed for auditions as if they were going to church. Today, everything is much more casual, so wear what suits you, and whatever makes you feel the most comfortable. Again, be yourself.

At musical auditions, there will always be a pianist on the premises, but always bring your own music. And make sure any changes in the music are clearly marked. Some actors hire their own accompanists. I don't think it's necessary, but if you feel better doing it and you can afford it, go ahead.

Something of a mythology has grown up around this whole matter of auditioning and casting in the theater and in Hollywood. Some people would lead you to believe that once you are out of school, getting ahead in the theater is largely a question of how active a sex life you're willing to have with producers and directors and others. This sort of thing does go on, of course, but

I would argue strongly against the idea that the only way to a successful career is by way of the producer's couch.

One problem facing the young actor today that simply didn't exist when I began acting is nudity. The situation may well change in a few years, but for the time being most of the inhibitions concerning sex and nudity on the stage and in the movies have been relaxed. I myself find it a little difficult to accept. I can't for the life of me see what nudity has to do with good acting. But perhaps if I were younger, I would feel differently. As it stands now, the mere thought of undressing onstage is horrifying to me. I know a few other actresses who are quite young who feel the same way.

It is, as I said, a matter of your own values, your own goals. I believe in the old cliché that you must be true to yourself. I say, don't do anything that compromises *your own* sense of balance. Trust your instinct!

We haven't yet touched upon the problem of what you do *after* the audition. What you don't do is to go home and sit by the phone or call your answering service every half hour. And you certainly don't call the producer's office. The waiting period between an audition and the day you find out if you've made the show or not can be an excruciating experience. If you can handle it, you've removed much of the pain from the acting experience.

The obvious advice is to try not to think about it.

Accept the fact that it's over and out of your hands. If you can do this, fine. If not, then indeed think about it. But not from the viewpoint of whether you're going to get the part or not, but from a clinical point of view. What did you do that was wrong? How can you correct it the next time? What can you do to improve yourself for the next time?

Like so many aspects of acting, an audition can be a valuable learning experience. Don't be easy on yourself. Judge yourself more harshly than the people who are supposed to judge you. Don't ignore your weaknesses. Isolate them and get rid of them. Put another way, this means that the best way to survive the audition you've just had is to start thinking about the next one as soon as possible.

·8·

PREPARATION

THE IMPACT OF STANISLAVSKI

What is important to me is not the truth outside myself . . . but the truth within myself.
—KONSTANTIN STANISLAVSKI, *My Life in Art*

The most talked about, and least understood, aspect of the acting process is preparation: what you do to prepare yourself emotionally, mentally, and physically for a new role. The most important book ever written on the subject is Konstantin Stanislavski's *An Actor Prepares*—the book from which we get the term "method acting."

This term, "method acting," has created great confusion in the United States ever since Stanislavski's theories were first introduced into this country in the early 1930's. This confusion has resulted, I think, because many people don't seem to understand what Stanislavski was trying to accomplish.

"Method acting," as I understand the term, is acting that relies principally on "inner technique." You're not simply creating the illusion of being angry or sad or happy onstage; you're actually feeling these emotions as well. You know what the character is supposed to feel and you can project that feeling.

This ability to generate emotional truth onstage has always been the hallmark of great acting. It began long before Stanislavski was born. Certain actors could do it. Others could not. Some actors, Laurette Taylor and Ethel Waters, for example, did it by instinct. For others, it was more of a conscious process. But because the process of projection was never clearly understood, it was ignored in the traditional methods of training actors. Instead, there were certain systems of acting: the Delsarte system, for instance, in which an actor was given certain gestures to make and poses to assume in order to convey emotional moments to the audience. The emphasis was purely on external technique.

You can visualize what these earlier styles of acting represented if you think of old-time melodramas such as *Uncle Tom's Cabin*. Today, any actor who makes grand gestures and roars out his lines is referred to as a "ham" and usually laughed at, but until the early 1920's in this country, this was considered the proper way to act. In formal training, it was not what you felt that was important; it was, rather, the motions and gestures you made onstage. A person who could "feel" onstage was considered to be endowed with some mysterious, God-given talent. It wasn't something you could learn.

Stanislavski refused to believe that the difference between a great actor and a mediocre actor was some mysterious power that one either possessed or didn't. He wanted to unlock the secret of this mysterious power or, as Lee Strasberg has explained, to take the "mystery" out of acting.

Stanislavski was really a kind of scientist. An actor creates a beautiful moment onstage. Stanislavski wanted to find out how this moment was created. He began by reading the notes and letters and books of great actors who had lived before him. He was constantly questioning the actors he directed at the Moscow Art Theater, the theater he co-founded. "What were you thinking about just then?" he might question an actor after a successful scene. "How did you create that moment? What was going through your mind?"

Eventually he realized that what he had initially suspected was true. Great acting didn't just happen. Each actor had a method of his own—either conscious or unconscious—for conveying reality. And here, I suppose, is where the term "method acting" actually originated.

But that was only the beginning of Stanislavski's work. Once he had established that every great actor had an individual method, and that this method could be analyzed and studied, he set out to organize all these methods into one rather loosely organized theory. And it was this approach to acting that subsequently became known as "the Stanislavski method" or simply, the "method."

In other words, there is no such thing as a "Stanislavski method" of acting. Stanislavski didn't originate a new system. What he did was to try to organize the methods used by great actors of the past into an approach that would enable the actor to develop his own "inner technique."

Lee Strasberg explained it well: "The Stanislavski method is nothing but the sum total of many great actors of the past, or the records and statements that they have left and of what we have seen in our own experience."

But even though the teachings of Stanislavski are not a "method" *per se*, there is a basic logic that underlies all the different theories that emerge in his writing.

He once asked a group of his acting students to walk up onstage, one by one, and sit on a chair for a few moments. Each student did what he was told. Most were a little uneasy and embarrassed and didn't know what to do next. But one young man sat down and immediately focused his attention on a workman who was building something offstage. He became fascinated by that workman, and it wasn't long before everyone in the audience was absorbed in watching the young actor watch the offstage workman.

This became one of the basic Stanislavskian principles. An audience will become interested in what you do onstage if you yourself are interested in what you're doing. An audience will feel what you do onstage, if you yourself *feel*. Of course, a big question still remained: How do you generate this feeling on your own?

Stanislavski's answer to this, in a very general sense, is: "The essential thing with dialogue of any kind is to find back of the words the experience and behavior that will give them life, so that they stem logically from the character on the stage. An actor must adjust himself to the role, and not the role to himself."

Here is the main thrust of Stanislavski's teaching— that the actor must be able and willing to subordinate himself to the dramatic situation in order to create reality through the character. Stanislavski wanted his actors to become "reincarnated" onstage. He wanted them to be reborn as the characters they were portraying. This, in his view, was the ultimate truth of acting.

Here lies one of the critical areas of the Stanislavskian

approach—the one element of the Stanislavski theory that has created the most controversy and misunderstanding. Is it necessary to actually *become* the character you are portraying, to actually "live the part"? Is this what acting is all about?

I would answer this way: Good acting, as Stanislavski pointed out throughout his writings, goes far beyond purely physical technique. The physical tools of acting must be guided by something inside the actor—an inner technique that embraces a variety of mental, psychological, and emotional processes.

Now the problem is how to trigger and control this inner technique. One way of achieving this is to assume what Stanislavski called the "second skin," to become as much as possible the character in the dramatic situation, to see life as he, the character, sees it, to respond as he, the character, responds. Remember, though, this is only *one* method of achieving the kind of emotional truth that Stanislavski talked about. The question isn't whether this particular method—"living the part"—is valid. The question is, does it work for you?

Then, too, there is always the danger of interpreting Stanislavski too literally. "Living the part" doesn't mean forgetting that you are onstage, that there is an audience. It doesn't mean that at all. This approach is only one direction an actor can take. It is not necessarily the absolute goal.

Stanislavski did not establish hard and fast rules. But

he emphasized that an actor must be able to do more than create a beautiful moment. He must be able to re-create that moment time and time again.

Here, really, is the essence of acting: Not to create a moment or two of brilliance onstage, but to repeat that moment over and over, night after night—through the knowledge of your craft, to find that moment *again*. What you do to find that moment again is *your* technique, *your* method. It doesn't really matter *how* you find it—only that you can count on it.

In the strict Stanislavskian sense of the word, I am not a "method" actress. As much as I would like to, I can't respond to every moment onstage through the character alone. I often have to go outside the character and into my own life. This is *my* method. If I have to cry, for example, I can't always feel the emotion through the character. I have to conjure up something in my own life that produces tears. But much of what Stanislavski wrote has helped me develop this method. And it is essential for you, as a young actor, to read Stanislavski. His ideas can help you develop your own technique.

Stanislavski's theories and the concept of method acting have come into disfavor among certain people in the theater simply because the ideas he introduced have been mistaught and misunderstood. Marlon Brando was the first of the so-called "method actors," and he has done remarkable work. It is fresh and real and vital. His acting has none of the bombast or the clichéd gesturing so common in classic acting technique.

Brando became a big success. He connected with his audiences, particularly with young people. But because he would sometimes pause between speeches and was accused of mumbling (although I don't think he did mumble as much as people thought), a lot of young actors thought, well, this is what method acting is. You mumble and you pause and you reflect, and you're *real*. So a good many young actors disregarded the basic elements of acting technique, as though Stanislavski had said to them: "Don't worry about being heard onstage or moving well. Just get out there and *feel* the part. The rest will come."

But Stanislavski never said that. And neither did Lee Strasberg nor Marlon Brando. Stanislavski, on the contrary, attached tremendous importance to what we think of as basic acting skills.

Sonia Moore wrote in *The Stanislavski System:* "Only the mastery of physical technique will assure the necessary freedom to permit an actor to execute a natural, truthful physical action and give himself to the experiences of the character. Few know or remember that Stanislavski said that the art of the theater is based on the union of the deep substance of the inner life and a beautiful, light, expressive form of it. The expressiveness of the art, the entire performance, depends on this union."

·9·

PREPARATION
THE ACTOR AND THE ROLE

When I first read a play, I usually see the woman in it—often I see her in bits and pieces, and then I have to join them up. There are always little bridges you have to keep crossing until they come.
—DAME EDITH EVANS, *Showcase*

I have never read—and no one has ever given me—an adequate explanation of exactly what happens between an actor and the character he is portraying.

In my career I have played an enormous variety of different character types: characters much younger than myself, such as Frankie Addams or Joan of Arc, and others much older than myself, such as Victoria Regina. I've played characters who were similar to me in outlook and personality, and characters who were the exact opposite. But in every instance, the basic problem has been the same: how to best use my instrument in order to make myself believable and effective as this other person—the character.

I agree with the Stanislavskian view that the actor must always adjust himself to the role. I also believe that this adjustment process is only successful when the actor understands his own technique and method well enough to know what he himself can contribute to make this character come alive.

One of the most common problems an actor faces is trying to establish some personal connection between himself and the character. Ideally, an actor should not take a role unless he believes in it—at least to some extent. But in building a career, this isn't always possible.

The important thing to consider when you are deciding whether to take a particular role is this: Is there something in it that interests you? This doesn't mean that you have to like or respect the character, or even that the play or movie script is on a high artistic level. Is there something in the role that you can bite into, something that will challenge you and teach you, something that *you* can believe in. I don't think you should worry too much over the size of the part. You can make just as much of an impression on an audience in a small part as you can in a big part.

Several years ago I went to the Bucks County Playhouse to play Theresa in Brendan Behan's *The Hostage*. It was a small part, but it contained, I thought, the spirit of the play. And it was one of the most enjoyable things I've ever done. Throughout my career I have been in many plays and movies that some people might have considered a waste of time. But in each of these roles, there was something that drew me to it, something that I could connect with.

The *reason* you take a particular role is secondary to the attitude you adopt once you begin preparing for it. Every actor has his own way of approaching a role. My method is to start out by saying, "Who is this character, and what can I do to get to know her?" I begin by reading the script, several times if necessary. I study details that say something to me personally. If it's a historical play or a period play, I do as much reading as I can. When I played in *The Lark*, I read everything I could get my hands on about Joan of Arc. I read the original trial records. I looked at hundreds of pictures of her. One fact stuck in my mind: On her first day in battle, she rode for hours in full armor. This small girl, a child, really—the strength and courage she had! How could I begin to project this?

I discovered complexities in her character. She wasn't

just a simple country girl. She had a sense of wit. She was humble, yes, but she also had an enormous ego. There was a wonderful contradiction between her pious humility and her excitement about being the leader of men in battle. And this is what I tried to get across in my characterization—all the intriguing complexities and ambivalences. I was tremendously interested in Joan as a person. This keyed the preparation process. It was all there in the script, too—beneath the surface—as in Tyrone Guthrie's phrase, like "echoes in a cathedral."

When I played Florence Nightingale in a television play called *The Holy Terror*, I began studying for the part by reading her biographies; eventually I read Florence Nightingale's notes about nursing.

Sometimes you do more than read. Before I did *Little Moon of Alban*, I read St. Vincent de Paul's writings on the Sisters of Charity. Then one day I visited some sisters in a House of Studies in Brooklyn. It was one of the most fascinating afternoons of my life. I marveled at the care that went into the way they dressed: the position of the sash, the cornet placed on the head just so. It all had special meaning, a sanctity of its own. I even asked one of the sisters why she had joined this particular order. Her answer was a revelation to me: "Because it assures me of heaven."

Another day that sticks in my mind is the afternoon I went to visit the Lexington School for the Deaf. I was getting ready to do a television production of *Johnny*

Belinda. I had already had some sign language instruction, but the thing that struck me as soon as I walked into the school was the noise. I had assumed that deaf-mutes were silent. But they're not. They force out sounds. And the face of a deaf-mute is a battlefield, with every muscle struggling to get sound across. And that was something that connected with me—how animated and how excited their expressions were.

The connection you make with the character can come in many ways. Sometimes, as it was with Ethel Waters in *The Member of the Wedding*, the identification between the character and the actor is already there. People often asked Ethel how she could cry night after night at the same moments in the play. Her answer was, the problem for her wasn't *how* to cry, but how *not* to cry—so much of the play reminded her of the sadness in her own life.

Some purely technical things can help in this process. In *The Member of the Wedding*, walking around barefoot and in a raggedy shirt took me back to my own childhood and helped put me in the spirit of the role. In the Broadway comedy *A Shot in the Dark* I played a French chambermaid, a Brigitte Bardot type, unlike any part I'd ever played. In this kind of role you can't very well do historical research. So I hung some pictures of Brigitte Bardot in my dressing room. I had my hair cut a special way. I designed a dress that reflected the character. And I began wearing perfume, something I'd never done before. I took pleasure in sensual things. These purely technical steps helped open my mind to the way this character viewed the world. It didn't mean that I agreed with her, only that I could understand her particular view of life.

In *Forty Carats* I had much the same problem. Ann Stanley was very different from most of the characters I'd played. I'd never thought of myself as a sophisticated leading-lady type, but when I accepted the role I had to develop a sense of believing in what this character represented. I began by looking through fashion magazines. I had my hair restyled. It wasn't my job as an actor to *judge* the way this particular character lived, only to *understand* and empathize with her situation.

It's surprising how little details can become the key to an entire characterization. In the television production of *Johnny Belinda* I worked with Christopher Plummer, a wonderfully resourceful actor, who called me one night extremely excited and said, "I'm going to play the doctor with an accent—a French-Canadian accent."

When Laurence Olivier did *The Power and the Glory* on television, he got a special pair of brown-tinted contact lenses to look more Mexican. Alan Arkin in the movie *The Heart Is a Lonely Hunter* planned the way the character would arrange things meticulously in a little toilet kit in his room. "I don't know if the audience notices these details," he said, "but they made this mute come true for me."

Sometimes an actor goes through a kind of identity crisis with a character. Few characters have ever given me as much difficulty as Frankie Addams, the adolescent in *The Member of the Wedding*, mostly, I guess, because it was my first big part. What finally put me on the right track was director Harold Clurman's advice. "Don't think about age," he told me. "Your age doesn't matter. You could be fifty and still play that part. If you put yourself in the circumstances and properly feel her pain, people are bound to think you're the right age." That's so true. Ellen Terry could give readings of Juliet when she was nearly seventy, and the audience would believe that she was fourteen. Old people act young, young people act old. It doesn't matter. Identify with what the character is feeling, and it will work.

As Sally Bowles in *I Am a Camera*, the problem was portraying a character who was everything that I was not: extroverted, outlandish, shocking. I can remember John van Druten, who directed as well as wrote the play, saying, "Forget about Sally. Just think about being outrageous."

But every actor, as I said earlier, has his own "method" of conjuring up reality through the character. A Stanislavskian purist would frown on any technique that didn't originate within the character. If you have to cry onstage, according to some actors, the emotional force must originate within the character and within that situation. In certain roles that is impossible. In Juliet's speeches, for instance, there are so many abrupt changes of emotional color, you simply must rely a great deal on purely physical things—voice and gesture—and you can't concern yourself with *feeling* every moment.

You have to find the balance. It would be wonderful if you could *feel* every moment in a play, but if you can't, you must "act" it out. I've seen actors just sit sometimes and brood over a moment to the point where it destroys the entire characterization. The thing to do if you're stuck is to think about it for a while, then quickly get up and try something. Try different approaches, different ways of saying a line. Often, through the physical projection—just by doing a thing—you make some inner connection.

I reject the idea of absolutes with acting. I disagree with those who insist that inner technique is useless to an actor, that an actor is a mechanic, a performer. And I disagree with those who are so inward, so psychologically oriented that they never get around to the business of acting, which is to get out onstage and give the audience their money's worth.

Acting, Stanislavski said—and we must never forget it—is a *union* of the inner and external technique.

·10·

PREPARATION
LEARNING LINES

*The best advice I can give to a young actor is this:
Learn your lines.*

—SPENCER TRACY

There are two basic approaches to learning lines. One
is to learn them all beforehand and go into rehearsal
with the part pretty well memorized. The other is to
learn the lines as you are "growing" with the character.
Ethel Waters and Christopher Plummer are two actors
who like to learn the lines as they go along. I like to go
into rehearsal with the lines already learned. I prefer

not to worry about the mechanics of the part when rehearsals start; this allows me the freedom to concentrate fully on the meaning.

I've been using the same system for memorizing lines
for years. I begin by reading the script over two or
three times. I underline my part. Then I figure out how
many pages I have to memorize and how much time I
have to work at it. I set up a schedule that divides the
number of pages into equal time segments. If I have
ten days to learn a hundred pages, I'll set up a schedule
of ten pages per day.

When it comes to the mechanics of learning the
lines, I tend to be a plodder. I read five lines, then
I repeat and repeat them until I know them. Next I
take five more lines, then I go back and review. I'm constantly reviewing and adding on. It's tedious work, but
I keep at it, a little at a time. Eventually, it all gets
learned.

I think the most difficult part to memorize I've ever
seen was that of the interrogator in *A Shot in the Dark*,
which I was in during 1961. The actor was William
Shatner, who later played the lead in the television series *Star Trek*. Bill's problem was that the role, besides
being very long, contained many speeches in which
he asked similar questions of different people with each
question phrased somewhat differently. There was also
a lot of legal terminology.

Bill worked by himself. He took each speech a little

at a time. He never let himself get rattled. He went about the job in a workmanlike, systematic way. Memorizing is as much a matter of skill as it is a matter of resolve and determination.

Some actors use tape recorders to help them memorize lines. Paul Muni did, and it helped him, he said, not only to memorize the part but to interpret it. I've never relied on this device, but I see no reason why it shouldn't work.

Writing out a part in longhand can be helpful. John Gielgud, for instance, writes out a new part in longhand two or three times. Some actors who get parts in television medical dramas write them out to better familiarize themselves with scientific terminology.

In any case, you're wise to do your actual memorizing work first thing in the morning, when your mind is fresh. I usually work for a few hours in the morning and then, just before going to bed, I go over the part once more. Sometimes I go to sleep with the feeling that I'm never going to learn the part. But when I get up the next morning, lo and behold, it has all somehow slipped into place.

Regardless of the system you use, and regardless of when you learn the lines, you must learn the meaning of them as you go along. This is especially important if you're working on a Shakespearean part. Whenever you sit down to learn any classical part, you should always have handy a dictionary or an authoritative guide to the play so that you can understand exactly what *every line in the play means.*

A final note about memorizing: Like everything else, it is a skill that can be improved through practice. And it is a skill that you should begin developing at an early age. You never know when you might find yourself with only two or three days in which to learn an entirely new part. Once you've developed this skill, you never lose it.

I've memorized more than fifty poems by Emily Dickinson. Now I have the joy of going over them in my mind from time to time, giving different colors to them, as if I were reading them in a book.

So I say, begin while you're young. Start out with the Shakespearean sonnets. Learn one a day. Then graduate to some of the better-known soliloquies. The point is not to work at it just once in a while, but on a regular basis—the way Sarah Bernhardt did. Bernhardt memorized purely for the sake of memorizing, the way a pianist would practice scales. If you practice memorizing, as little as a half hour a day for a year, you'll have reached a point where you can memorize any part in only a few days.

·11·

REHEARSALS
THE ACTOR'S LABORATORY

*In the production of a good play with a good cast and
a knowing director a kind of banding together occurs;
there is formed a fraternity whose members share a
mutual sense of destiny.*
    —ARTHUR MILLER, "The American Theatre,"
Holiday magazine, reprinted in *The Passionate Playgoer*

The word *rehearse* comes from the Middle English
word *rehersen*, which means to reharrow or dig up the
earth again. That's what actors do at rehearsals. We
dig into the same earth, again and again. Through this

process, we enrich ourselves. We gain a better understanding of who we are and what we are trying to do. I, for one, love to rehearse. It's the thing I like best about being an actress.

"The rehearsal," Margaret Leighton, the great English actress, said, "is where the actor can make a bloody fool of himself."

That's true. But only if the rehearsal is carried out in the right spirit and under the right atmosphere. Rehearsals are laboratories. In rehearsals the actor can experiment, try things he wouldn't dream of doing in front of an audience.

The average rehearsal time for a Broadway play is from three to three and a half weeks. I wish it were longer. When I played Juliet at Stratford, Canada, we had seven weeks of rehearsal. We worked on three plays simultaneously, but it wasn't as confusing as you might think. Nobody had three major parts. A longer rehearsal period gives you a chance to grow into your role at a more natural, more gradual pace. It also helps the members of the acting company to get used to one another. I don't think a Broadway production, for example, really hits its stride until about a month after it opens. It usually takes that long to establish a rhythm and continuity.

In summer stock the rehearsal period is much shorter —a week at most. In school and community acting groups the rehearsal period is usually spread over a lengthy period of time, with the schedule becoming more intensive a week or so before opening night.

No matter how much rehearsal time you have, however, the basic rehearsal procedure is the same. You generally begin the first day by just reading through the play or by listening to the director give you his feeling of what you should be trying to do.

I've worked three times with Harold Clurman. Each time he spent the first two days exploring the mystery of the story for us. Harold usually gives the cast his vision of the play in such an exciting way that the cast's anticipation grows and grows—he arouses your own yearning to get on with the story, to get on with the characterization, to such a point that you are eager to begin.

After this introduction, you start right in with "blocking" or "staging" rehearsals. Here you go through the play line by line. You note every movement in your script. You know exactly where you should be standing and what you should be doing at every moment in the play. Blocking rehearsals are tedious and slow moving. But you must remain alert. Few things infuriate a director more than to see an actor forget basic blocking instructions late in the rehearsal schedule. You should always study blocking instructions the evening of the day they've been given.

After blocking, you begin rehearsing the play in small sequences. It's here, if there is time and if the director is flexible, that an actor can try different things. You may do a scene differently five or six times or even more. Maybe you'll change some blocking. This is usually the most intensive part of the rehearsal period. You're hammering out the shape and focus of your role.

Generally, midway through the second week run-throughs begin. In a run-through the cast tries to act through the play without interruption. Occasionally, if there's a major mix-up, you may have to go over a particular scene, but usually there are no corrections or comments until afterward, when the cast gathers around the director to hear his evaluation. "Come in a little faster on your entrance," a director might say to one actor. Or to another: "A little more emotion on that last exit."

At some point in the run-throughs, you have your first technical rehearsal, that is, with the actual scenery and props. Up to now you've been working on either an empty stage or in a rehearsal hall with makeshift props and scenery. Then, before opening night, there's always a final run-through with makeup, lights, and costumes.

This is as good a place as any to discuss makeup. As lighting techniques in the theater improve, the technology of makeup changes, and the newer materials, luckily, are much less punishing to the skin than the grease sticks used when I first started. Many younger actors and actresses use very little makeup, particularly for movies. But to get by without using much makeup, you have to take very good care of your skin.

And you should learn about makeup when you're starting out. The best way to learn about it, is to get some and try using it. A basic makeup kit, on sale in many drugstores, shouldn't cost more than $12. You begin by finding out how your skin reacts to different colors. My skin, for instance, tends to absorb makeup, so if I'm to have any color at all, I need a dark brown base.

Then, too, your makeup requirements change according to the role, the lighting at the theater in which you are working, and the medium you're working in. Makeup is more crucial for live television, for instance, than it is for the movies. I suggest that you get a book on makeup from the library—there are several good ones—and practice at home. Remember, the more you can do for yourself as an actor, the more confidence you'll develop.

In the movies or in a television series you rarely rehearse the script as a whole. The usual procedure is to rehearse a short scene without the cameras until the director is satisfied you can get through it. But don't get the idea that because you're working in film you can do a scene an infinite number of "takes" until it's just right. Takes are expensive, and a good director doesn't like to repeat them unnecessarily—particularly for a television movie, when the budget and schedule are limited.

Anna Sokolow, a dancer and choreographer who was dance director at the Actors Studio when I was working there, used to complain that the first half hour of a rehearsal was usually a waste of time. "The trouble," she would tell us, "is that you're still thinking about something else when you first come in." She added, "If you're serious about your work here, you have to get ready for the rehearsal even before you arrive."

It's a good point to remember. The moment you walk into a rehearsal hall, your mind should be filled with nothing else but the sense of what you're doing. It's not the time to be thinking about politics or school-work or dates. Every minute of the rehearsal should be devoted to the rehearsal and nothing but the rehearsal.

Certain rules apply to all rehearsals, no matter where they take place. The cardinal rule is punctuality. To show up even a few minutes late for a rehearsal is to show disrespect for your director, your fellow actors, and your profession. Few things are worse for the morale of a company than to have one or two actors constantly keeping everyone else waiting.

Equally important is your attitude and behavior once you're there. When I did my first Broadway play, *It's a Gift*, and didn't know any better, I brought a book with me to read during the rehearsal. I didn't realize how much this bothered the director and what an insult it was to the other actors. I got fired from that production, incidentally, and it was only because the playwright, Curt Goetz, spoke on my behalf to the director that I was rehired.

In school dramatic activities you may be tempted to bring your homework to rehearsal. Don't. Think of what a school football coach would say if his players did their history while he was teaching them new plays!

True, you may have quite a bit of work to do—maybe even an important exam in the morning—but if you're serious about acting, you must make the necessary sacrifices. You have to make time *after* the rehearsal, even if it means giving up a movie or passing up a party, to complete your studying.

If you have only a small part in the production, you can still involve yourself. There is a fascination in watching a play take shape, in watching individual actors work out their problems. You can learn so much at a rehearsal merely by being attentive and observant. And don't be too proud to work on the purely physical aspects of the production—the sets, the lights, the costumes. The more you learn about the theater in its entirety, the more you can bring to your craft. Many successful Broadway and television directors started out in the theater as stage managers.

Obviously, noise and distractions at a rehearsal must be kept to a minimum. But this doesn't mean that the atmosphere must be rigidly silent or deadly dull. I like to see an easygoing, very relaxed atmosphere at rehearsals. You're all there to work, but it should be fun, too. I like actors who are responsive to what goes on, who laugh if another actor has done a funny piece of business, who applaud if a scene has gone well.

Don't be afraid to dress outlandishly at rehearsals. If you have an original costume idea for the character you are portraying, try it out. Similarly, if you've come up with some crazy scheme to work a prop, give it a try. A good director will always encourage his actors to be inventive.

The key figure in rehearsals, of course, is the director. There's no escaping the fact that what you ultimately do onstage will be determined by the sort of relationship you have with the director during the rehearsal period.

I am a traditionalist. I think the director *must* be the final authority, not the actor. As an actor you have the right to thrash things out and talk about things you find upsetting, but in the end you must give in to the director's will. Acting is a group experience. The director is concerned with how the play works as a whole, not only with the problems of individual actors.

My first experience with a director in the professional theater was terrible. I was convinced I couldn't begin to do the sort of things he was asking of me onstage. I became sullen and uncooperative.

I realize now how wrong I was. Badgering a director accomplishes absolutely nothing. Sometimes it's hard to follow a direction you don't agree with or can't feel, but it doesn't hurt as much as you may think to trust the director. Not that you always compromise! If you feel deeply that you are right, you don't have to compromise. But you do have to make a choice, one way or the other; and once you make the choice, follow it through.

I remember arguing with Abe Burrows over the first scene in *Forty Carats*. In the scene I was stranded at a café in a small Greek town. Abe wanted me to strew a lot of Kleenex all over the table. It was a funny touch, but I'm basically a neat person. I felt the character was neat, too, and wouldn't mess up a table like that. This may seem like a silly conflict, but these are the kinds of disagreements that can create tension in a cast. As it happened, we compromised. There was Kleenex, but not quite as much as Abe wanted.

No two directors work quite the same way or relate in the same way to actors. I never worked with Arthur Hopkins, who directed John Barrymore's Hamlet, but actors who did say he was marvelous. He would sit in the audience and never say a word until afterward, but you always knew he was there. He'd let the life of a play grow on its own, and work from there.

John van Druten was wonderful to work with in *I*

Am a Camera. He was like a child watching the play unfold. He was a wonderful audience. If he liked something, he would scream for joy. If he loved what you did, you knew about it. If he didn't like what you did, you knew about that, too.

I like directors who are open to suggestions from the actors. In *East of Eden,* for example, Elia Kazan would gather us around before the shooting and say, "Okay, let's talk about what we're going to do."

But you can't always count on getting a director with whom you can feel sympathetic. As I've said, it's up to you to make the relationship work. A number of times I've watched established actors annihilate a new director over some small, insignificant point. In almost every instance, the whole project suffers. The morale of an acting company is fragile. Nothing depletes it more quickly than a feud between the director and the leading man or woman.

But let's not dwell unnecessarily on the negative aspects of the rehearsal period. As I've already said, the rehearsal is the place for you, as an actor, to discover yourself and grow—and you will if you go into it with this in mind.

Quite often, some remarkable acting moments come alive during a rehearsal. Once in an acting class—which is similar in a way to the rehearsal atmosphere—I was acting out a scene from *The Glass Menagerie* with another actor. This was the scene in which the Gentleman Caller whirls Laura around and accidentally knocks the little glass unicorn off the table. The way the scene is written, Laura picks up the broken figurine, smiles, and pretends not to be bothered by it. Well, when I picked up the unicorn, I got a little cut in my finger. I don't know whether it was the cut or the fact that I was so caught up in the scene, but anyway, I began to cry. The other actor didn't stop the scene. We continued, reciting the lines just as they were, except that a new dimension was added to the scene, the fact that I was trying to stop crying. It gave the scene a richer sense of reality. And the effect on the class was amazing.

In *The Member of the Wedding* I remember the scene in which Frankie chases her cousin, John Henry, around the table. Here again, I was so caught up with what I was doing in one rehearsal that I screamed at him, "You little midget!" And Harold Clurman clapped his hands and said, "Wonderful, leave it in."

This is what I mean by discovery, and what Margaret Leighton meant when she talked about an actor making a "fool of himself" at a rehearsal. In order to succeed at anything, you have to be prepared to fail many times. It's too much to expect of an actor that he be prepared to fail in public, so he must be willing to do adventurous things during rehearsal. Most of the things you try may not work at all, but if everyone is locked into the

same adventurous spirit, you'll never fear being embarrassed.

William Faulkner was once asked which of his novels
was his favorite. *"The Sound and the Fury,"* he replied,
"because it was my greatest failure."

Yes. No one succeeds without many failures. Rehearsals give the actor that chance.

·12·

OPENING NIGHT

I kept saying to myself, as I have done on every first night since, "Why am I doing this? Why didn't I try to do something else?" I would have been glad of an earthquake or some other great calamity that would stop people from coming in or me from going on.
— ETHEL BARRYMORE, talking about the opening of
Captain Jinks, from *Memories*

Opening night in the professional theater—and I'm thinking primarily of Broadway—is a nightmare. It warrants no comparison with the sort of opening nights you'll probably be facing over the next few years. A Broadway opening may be glamorous for the audience, but for an actor it is the ordeal of ordeals.

If all you had to worry about was doing your job, it wouldn't be such a problem. But so much hangs on an opening night performance. A good night, good reviews, good audience reaction—they hold the promise of steady employment and who knows what else. If things go badly, it usually means weeks of backbreaking work gone up in smoke.

Nothing would gratify me more than to see Broadway change its opening night philosophy, so that an opening would be just another performance. Let the critics come at different times during the first couple of weeks. Let the audiences decide if the play is worthwhile or not. I suspect that many wonderful plays have been lost because the opening night performance—that *one* performance—didn't come off well.

But let's forget Broadway for the time being and talk about first performances in general. For me, the preparation process for the opening begins several days before. I realize that the time for experimentation is over. I have to pull the characterization together so it will be finished and reasonably polished. My lines are solidly entrenched in my memory. I'm sure of my staging. I'm aware of possible problem areas—a difficult stage move or a troublesome speech. I do extra work on these problem areas. I know that regardless of how sure I am of what I'm doing, I'm going to be ridiculously nervous on opening night. I'm determined not to make the problem any greater than it's going to be under normal circumstances.

Most of the time, unless something unexpected has happened (maybe a leading actor has taken sick), there is no rehearsal on the day of the opening night. In any case, I do my best to get a good night's sleep the night before. I try to arrange my schedule so that on the day of the opening I can take things easy and relax.

Some actors will tell you not to even think about the play until you get to the theater that evening. I don't agree. Louis Armstrong once said that whenever he had an engagement in the evening, he would spend the whole day thinking about the first note.

Now there is a difference between "thinking about the first note" and worrying yourself to death. Early in your career you ought to differentiate between productive concern about what you have to do and unnecessary worry.

I generally stay around the house, or if we're on the road, at the hotel on the day of the opening night. Maybe I'll go over the notes of the last rehearsal or walk through on my own some of the sequences the director talked about. Maybe I'll say the part aloud one last time. Iris Warren used to advise actors to whisper their part to themselves as a way of getting command of it.

What you eat that day is extremely important. You don't want to act on an empty stomach, but at the same time you don't want to eat so much that you'll be sluggish. I generally eat a light supper around four thirty. Avoid coffee; it can put you on edge. Also keep away from milk and milk products; they coat the throat with a layer of phlegm that can cause problems onstage. Tea with honey is excellent. I always keep a small electric coil in my dressing room so that I can make my own tea or hot bouillon between acts.

Usually you'll be expected to show up at the theater no later than an hour and a half before the curtain. I try to arrive even earlier. The last thing I want to do is to feel pressured or rushed in any way.

When I get to the theater and sign in, I go immediately to my dressing room. I make sure that all my costumes are in order. Then I make sure of all my hand props. I go out onstage and check for myself that everything is in its proper place. These things are the stage manager's or propman's responsibility, but double-checking doesn't mean I don't trust his competence. It means that I believe everything an actor is involved with onstage is *his* responsibility. When something goes wrong, when a prop isn't in the right place, the actor is the one who ultimately suffers.

Once everything is checked out, I go back to my dressing room to make up and dress. In school there are generally a couple of people responsible for makeup. But not in the professional theater. You have to do it yourself.

I like to be in costume and makeup at least a half hour before the curtain. Then I like to just sit by myself in the dressing room and think about what I'm supposed to be doing when I get out onstage for the first time.

Sometimes there's commotion backstage on an opening night: lots of going from dressing room to dressing room, wishing good luck, and occasionally the exchanging of small gifts. Personally, I wish it wouldn't go on. One of the ways I deal with my nervousness is to sit there and tell myself, "Well, there's nothing really unusual about tonight. You're going to go out there and do what you did in rehearsal." But every time someone wishes me luck, it reminds me again that this *isn't* just another performance.

Actors get "psyched up" for performances in different ways. Some actors do vocal exercises. Others do the little stretching exercises you learn in dance class.

What I do is mainly determined by the part. In *Forty Carats*, I was supposed to be upset and disoriented in the very first scene, so I let myself get nervous. When I did *The Country Wife*, director George Devine wouldn't let me sit alone in my dressing room. He wanted me to get into a spirit of mischief. He encouraged me to go around backstage and talk to everyone. I even learned to juggle three oranges as a way to help me relax.

You can always expect some form of opening night jitters. And frankly, I am the last person to give advice on how to deal with this. On some opening nights I become not just nervous, but almost frozen. My technique gets me through it, but I don't really feel anything. I've never been able to figure out why it happens in certain plays and not others. In *I Am a Camera* I had the usual jitters beforehand, but as soon as I got out onstage, I felt warm and sunny, and everything just flowed. In *The Lark* I began like a cube of ice but relaxed as the play moved on. Sometimes all I want to do before I go out is sit down and cry. The only thing that forces me out onstage is the realization that I have no choice and the knowledge that technically I am in command of my part.

There is no real solution; you just deal with it. What saves you is the realization that a lot of other people go through the same thing. I was once in a film, *Harper*, with Paul Newman. Few actors are more successful than Paul, yet before each little scene, he'd go over to the side, get a towel, and wipe the sweat off his palms.

What every actor fears, not just on opening night but at any performance, is that something will go wrong: a prop won't work, a door won't open, an actor —maybe you—will lose his way in the part.

The most common form of unrehearsed stage incident is the dropped line. Curiously, it doesn't usually
happen on opening night, but sometimes weeks after
you've been doing the part. In *The Member of the
Wedding* one night I completely forgot an entire sequence of lines. I still don't know what really happened. Ethel Waters and Brandon de Wilde were onstage, and I'd just said the line about my older brother
and his fiancée being the two most beautiful people I
had ever known, and then everything suddenly went
blank.

I panicked. The prompter was giving me the line,
but I couldn't hear her because there were oceans
roaring in my ears. Ethel did her best to ad-lib us out
of the dilemma. "What ails you, child," she kept saying.
"What ails you?" But I couldn't speak. I walked to the
mirror and looked at myself and began pulling at my
hair. But it still didn't help. Ethel finally saved the day
by skipping ahead several lines. "Come on. Less have
a game of three-handed bridge," she said, and led me
to the table. From that point on, I was okay.

A similar thing happened one night about six months
after *Forty Carats* had opened. I was doing a scene with
Marco St. John. Suddenly I couldn't think of anything
to say. Fortunately, I was a little calmer this time. I
headed over toward the wings and without stepping out
of character I cued Marco with my eyes. Marco became
aware of the problem, and we ad-libbed a line or two
until I got back on the track.

Nobody knows what causes these temporary mental blackouts onstage, but they seem to happen to every actor. I know of no way to prevent them; you can only prepare for them by convincing yourself that when they do happen, you'll somehow survive.

No matter what happens onstage, don't let it knock you off stride for the rest of the performance. Stay with the character as much as possible. If you fluff one line, forget about it instantly. Most of the time the audience won't notice what's happened. In *Little Moon of Alban* there is a scene in which the little boy who later dies is supposed to make a wish on the birthday cake and blow out the candles. One of the candles was a trick candle; it wasn't supposed to go out. Its continuous light was to be a symbolic moment that prepared the audience for the boy's eventual death. A couple of times the propman put *all* regular candles on the cake, and all the candles went out. When this happened, we simply made an overly big fuss over the wish. That gave the moment some irony.

Sometimes, though, you can't conceal what's happened. I worked with June Havoc in New Orleans in a play called *The Women*. In an early scene a group of us had to sit down at a bridge table. One night the leg of one of the chairs happened to be on top of the opening between two components of the turntable platform. When the actress sat down, the leg of the chair went through the opening and she fell to the floor. To make matters worse, in the play she is pregnant.

When it happened, we all stayed in character, as if the fall were part of the script. "Are you all right, dear?" we asked. "Are you sure?" We put the chair upright and rearranged ourselves. Then it happened a second time. The audience broke up. There was nothing we could do but set the chair up again and in spite of our embarrassment plunge ahead. Within moments, the accident onstage had been forgotten.

One of the classic stage stories concerns the actor who was supposed to kill himself. On cue he reached into a drawer for a gun. The gun wasn't there. "All right," he ad-libbed, "I'll knife myself to death." But there was no knife. Finally, in desperation, he looked at the audience, took hold of his head with both hands, and wrenched his neck around. "There," he screamed. "I've broken my damn neck." And he fell to the floor. Dead!

What it comes down to, finally, is that the incident itself, when it happens onstage, is never as horrifying as you imagine it will be. You should not concern yourself too much with the possibility of its happening.

These little incidents onstage become major problems only when you allow them to get away from you. Good actors always stay in control. An actor once made an entrance from the wrong side of the stage during a performance with Edwin Booth's father, Junius Booth. When the actor apologized, Booth said: "It makes no difference to me. Just come in. I'll find you."

·13·

THE MOVIES AND TV

He (D. W. Griffith) achieved what no other known man has ever achieved. To watch his work is like being witness to the beginning of melody, or the first conscious use of the lever or the wheel; the emergence co-ordination, and first eloquence of language . . . the birth of an art. And to realize that this is all the work of one man.

—JAMES AGEE, *Agee on Film*

Most young American actors I know want to become movie stars. I can't blame them. Apart from the money (you can make more money in a single film than you can working all year on Broadway), the opportunities in film and on television are much better than in the theater. More people see one hit movie in a year than all the plays on Broadway put together.

It used to be fashionable for stage actors to thumb their noses at films, but not any more. As for me, I've always been fascinated by film.

The stage is still my first love though. I grew up with it. I was trained for it. Nothing can replace for me the immediacy of working in front of an audience. But I've always liked working in movies. I don't consider it an inferior form of acting. In certain respects, it is more difficult. It requires even more concentration than a stage performance.

When it comes to inner technique and basic role preparation, the acting process is pretty much the same in both films and the stage. The big difference is in style and in some of the environmental conditions that separate the two mediums.

The first film I ever made was the screen version of *The Member of the Wedding*. It gave me a lot of trouble.

"Say it quieter," Fred Zinneman, the director, used to say to me over and over. "You don't have to project so much. Take it easy. Be natural."

Film acting, I quickly discovered, is much more precise than stage acting. The movie or television camera is like a lie detector. It has no ear, but it records thoughts. It wants to see those thoughts. "If you stay in front of that camera long enough," Lionel Barrymore once said, "it will not only show what you had for breakfast, but who your ancestors were."

Another big difference is pacing. In the theater you prepare yourself mentally so that at curtain time you're set to plow ahead for two and a half straight hours. In the movies the work is piecemeal. You may spend five or six days on a sequence that runs only a few pages in the script. And you just don't do a scene once. The basic approach to film making has changed little since the pioneering days of D. W. Griffith. Each scene is shot several times, each time from a different angle. Last of all are the close-ups. I'll never know why they shoot the close-ups last. That's when you want to do your best work, and also the time that it's most difficult to generate feeling—by then, of course, you're exhausted.

The technical demands of film acting make it a difficult medium in which to apply pure Stanislavskian principles. You can't rely entirely on involvement with the character. You need a technique, a strong acting technique. You never really act the role as a whole, only in short segments.

If there is any secret to film acting, I would say it lies in the ability to relax and to concentrate. On a stage, with the lights coming at you, you play to almost a wall of blackness. Beyond the first or second row of the theater, you can't really see much. It isn't difficult to concentrate. On a movie or television set, however, everything is open. Cameras are all around. Technicians are everywhere. If you're on a street, there's noise and a lot of spectators—a million things to get your mind off your acting. Marlon Brando has a marvelous power of concentration on a movie set. He even puts plugs in his ears to cut out extraneous noise. James Dean was another actor who could really involve himself with his role and never allow the extraneous activity around the set to affect his concentration.

One of the most interesting things about working on *East of Eden* was the peculiar chemistry that developed between Jimmy and Raymond Massey. Raymond played his father in the film. Jimmy had a habit of swearing on the set, and it used to upset Raymond. Raymond liked Jimmy and wanted to like him more, but he couldn't help but be put off by the language. This ambivalance carried over into the movie itself, where the father had a similar kind of love-hate feeling for his son. Jimmy sensed this, I think, and either consciously or unconsciously kept on swearing throughout the shooting.

The working day in the movies is very long. You usually start at eight or eight thirty in the morning. If you're shooting on location or have a complicated hairdo, you may have to get there much earlier. But the most tiring part of the day is the pace. It's very much the same as in blocking rehearsals, only worse. You work for a few minutes. Then you stop and wait for the cameras to get lined up again. Then you start again, and then stop. You work up to an emotional pitch, and then you have to cool down. You have to pace yourself so that at the end of the shooting day you're just as strong as you were in the morning.

You *must* learn to relax during those frequent periods between shootings. Many actresses do needlepoint. Some read or work crossword puzzles. Anything that will occupy your mind without dimming your concentration is good.

In a strict technical sense, you don't have nearly the freedom of movement in film that you do on the stage. If you have to make an entrance onstage, you can vary your position a little bit one way or the other. In a film you must, as they say, "hit your mark." Tape on the floor tells you exactly where you must stand. Some actors, in order to make sure they won't miss their mark, put little sandbags on the floor. That way, they can tell with their feet whether they're in the right position. Experienced actors develop almost a sixth sense when it comes to "hitting the mark."

The particular demands of film acting were brought home to me dramatically during the filming of an episode in the television series *The Name of the Game*, in which I played a psychologist. The climactic scene takes place in a hospital. A runaway girl has taken an overdose of drugs and has just been brought into the intensive care unit. The girl's mother, her father, Robert Stack, and I are standing in the observation room, watching as the doctors try desperately to save the girl's life. It's no use. The girl dies before our eyes.

This is a strong scene and emotionally not difficult to act. The first time they shot it, it was simple to cry. The second shot was easy, too. But by the time they got around to the close-ups, there was no one left on the set but the four of us. The set had been stripped. We were simply standing with nothing but our imaginations to work with. I felt cried out. It was already evening. We'd been working since early that morning. I was exhausted, and I didn't think there was any way I could act out that final close-up scene.

But you don't say to a movie director, "I can't do it now, can't we wait until tomorrow?" There is no one you can appeal to except yourself. So you reach back and you concentrate and concentrate and put everything out of your mind and conjure up emotion, and somehow you get through the scene.

No, there's nothing easy about film acting. And it isn't necessarily less creative than stage acting. Just as in theater rehearsals, some wonderful moments can take place on a movie set. A good example is a television movie, *How Awful About Allan,* which I made in the winter of 1969 with Tony Perkins. Tony played my brother. He'd been blinded in a fire which had killed our father. I'd been bedeviling him throughout the film, and in one of the last scenes he discovers what I've been doing. We are in the kitchen together and the script called for me to beat his chest and scream as the scene fades out. The director told us to keep going with the scene until we heard "cut." So we continued with it, improvising. Then, instinctively, I stopped screaming and beating and simply slumped against his chest and started to cry. And Tony put his arms around me and started calming me down. We created a whole new moment—one the scriptwriter hadn't thought of.

Everything else being equal, I think it's easier to be first trained for the stage and then try movies than to grow up making movies and then try to make the transition to the stage. The accomplished actor can act well in both mediums—Anne Bancroft, Lee J. Cobb, George C. Scott, Henry Fonda, Jason Robards, to name just a few. But the demands are great in both.

Film acting has done much to make me a better stage actress. The main thing I had to learn and am still learning is to keep searching inside myself for what is truthful, to expose my innermost feelings. Before the camera, there must be no pretense, only truth.

The truly great film personalities acted without a shred of pretense. Jimmy Cagney, Clark Gable, Gary Cooper, Humphrey Bogart, Spencer Tracy, Bette Davis. What we see on screen is so true, so simple, so natural. You understand what Griffith meant when he said:

"The camera opens and shuts, opens and shuts with equal time—so half of everything you do isn't seen. Then take away the sound [he was talking about silent movies], and you lose another quarter. What's left on screen is a quarter of what you felt or did—therefore, your expression must be four times as deep and true as it would be normally to come over with full effect to your audience."

Stanislavski might well have written the same advice.

·14·

THE OTHER ACTOR

If you don't take care of one another, nobody else will.
—ELIA KAZAN

Once when I was studying at the Actors Studio, a group
of us in a play called *Sundown Beach* went up to Westport, Connecticut, to give a performance at the Westport Playhouse. It was summer and because we had
arrived early, some of the cast went down to the beach.
One girl got extremely sunburned on the legs. It wasn't
sun poisoning, but it was close.

The director, Elia Kazan, was furious. Not with the actress, but with the rest of us. "You have to look after one another," he said. "You shouldn't have let this girl get so much sun. If you don't take care of one another, nobody else will."

There was a time when an acting company was very much like a family. It was the time of the traveling troupe. But that era is gone, and with it, I think, a rather wonderful way of life for the actor, despite the hardships these companies sometimes experienced. This isn't to say a group feeling doesn't develop in acting companies today. It does. Even on a ten-day film shooting, you can get attached to the people you work with. And that's the problem. You get attached to people, and then you're saying good-bye. For me, this is one of the most painful aspects of acting.

I don't know of any acting school in this country that stresses graciousness. I wish it could be taught. I wish more actors would learn it. Simple things such as a warm hello to your fellow actors, a "thank you" to the prompter when he's fed you a line, or some appreciation toward the production people. All these can mean so much.

Sometimes it's not easy. Acting attracts a wide variety of personalities. Some actors are by nature insecure, hostile, rude, or bullish. But no matter what the other actor does, you must not lose your own sense of balance.

One of the worst things you can do as an actor, as

far as I'm concerned, is to put pressure on another actor who is having trouble with a part. In *The Member of the Wedding* it took Brandon de Wilde several weeks before he was contributing anything. Some of us were getting a little nervous, but Harold Clurman, the director, told us just to be patient and understanding, that the boy would find himself in his own way and in his own time. How right he was! An astonishing transformation came over Brandon in the last week before opening. I don't think it could have happened if the rest of us in the cast had pressured him in any way.

This sympathy and understanding shouldn't end the moment you get onstage. A good actor makes the people around him look good. He's not worried that the audience might be paying more attention to somebody else than to him. One of the most unselfish actors I know is Dirk Bogarde. I worked with him in *Little Moon of Alban*. It was a joy from start to finish, for Dirk is an actor who really listens onstage. He is so completely fused with his part, so interesting in and of himself that he literally forces you to get involved, too.

Walter Matthau is another actor who is a pleasure to work with—again, because onstage you know the two of you are working *together*, not against each other.

On the other hand, there are actors whose behavior would test the patience of Job. "Problem" actors fall into specific categories. There's the actor who's constantly complaining: about the director, about the sets, about the costumes. If you listen to him for very long, you become convinced that the show is never going to make opening night. Then there's the actor with a capital A—so caught up in his own situation, with the idea of being an *actor*, that he can't be bothered with anything else.

I worked once with an actress whose dressing room was close to the stage. She liked to recite her lines before she went out onstage, and you could hear her on the stage. We complained to her often, but she always seemed to forget. She was so immersed in her own situation, it never dawned upon her that she was inconveniencing the rest of us.

You also run into actors who take themselves so seriously they threaten your safety. In some plays you have to be dragged around onstage and sometimes there are staged fights. If an actor doesn't realize that you're supposed to *simulate* the violence, you can get hurt. When this happens, he simply has to be told that he can't manhandle you. And if he doesn't listen, you ought to go to the director.

The theater is filled with actors who must be the center of attention in every scene. Many of them have a way of moving upstage, that is toward the back of the stage, so that you find it necessary to act with your back to the audience. This happens to me from time to time, and when it does, I try not to play the same game. Your back can be very effective, provided the line is delivered correctly and you don't lose concentration.

In any case, nothing is accomplished if you, as an actor, meet another actor's disrespect or lack of consideration with similar behavior. Often he's behaving that way because of his own insecurity. If you act hostile in any way, it's only going to compound the problem.

An actor may be difficult, egotistical, rude, insulting, or even vicious, but if he's a great actor, you may be able to learn something from him.

Finally, it's always wise to refrain from discussing other actors in the company. There is a little of the gossip in all of us, but gossiping is one of the things you should discipline yourself against.

To repeat: Where your fellow actors are concerned, you should go beyond the golden rule.

·15·

GETTING STARTED

I must find new actors for my films among those who do not have—or not yet—success, among those who still have a passion, an anxiety, a violence that they will almost always lose later. . . . In short, I try to catch my actors at the moment when they are still, or again, human.

— ELIA KAZAN, "A Natural Phenomenon," *Cahiers du Cinema*

The situation for the young actor today in America is far different from what it was in the late 1940's when I first began in the professional theater.

In some respects, it's better. Working conditions have improved. Air transportation has made touring much easier. The pay is better, although the rise in pay scales hasn't really kept pace with the rising wage scales of other professions. And actors, generally speaking, enjoy a higher status than they did twenty-five years ago.

During the early days of Hollywood, an actor couldn't even get a first-class hotel room. And twenty-five years ago people would have scoffed at the idea that a movie star, such as Ronald Reagan or George Murphy, would have a future in American politics.

Since more actors go to college today than ever before, the young actors of this generation tend to be more intellectually and socially aware, more concerned with current events, more caught up in the mainstream of our times than actors of other eras. Theater life is no longer as isolated as it was.

In terms of opportunity, it's difficult to make comparisons. There was far more legitimate theater work when I began. More plays were being produced on Broadway. More plays toured. More summer theaters were in operation. From 1945, when I first came east, until 1950, when I got my first big role—Frankie Addams in *The Member of the Wedding*—I played in ten different Broadway plays. None of them was a success, but the experience I gained during the rehearsals— working with different actors and different directors— all of it was irreplaceable.

Today, unless you are extremely successful, it's impossible to make a living solely as an actor on Broadway or in off-Broadway productions. Almost all actors in New York supplement their income somehow: in movies, in soap operas, or in television commercials. There simply aren't enough plays. And the plays that open usually don't run long enough for an actor to support himself, let alone his family, in a city as expensive as New York.

On the other hand, there are many more regional repertory companies today. Nearly every large American city has its own resident theater company. These companies don't pay a tremendous amount of money, only enough to live on, provided you don't have too large a family to support. The important thing is that these companies guarantee you steady work, at least forty weeks a year.

I've always believed that experience is the actor's only real teacher—actual stage experience, in front of a live audience, or screen experience, with a professional group of film makers. Acting classes and acting studios are marvelous learning laboratories, valuable to an actor's growth, but nothing takes the place of actual experience.

One place to get this experience is in college. A formal education is important. If I had it to do again, I would definitely go to college. More and more colleges now offer interesting theater and drama courses, and nearly every college has its own resident theater company. The quality of a university theater program depends on many things, mainly the teachers and directors. Famous names on the faculty are no guarantee that the overall instuction and the general atmosphere will be helpful to your growth as an actor. The thing to look for, in my opinion, is a program that concentrates less on theory and more on the actual work itself. You can learn more about Shakespeare by acting out a role than you can by listening to a Shakespearean scholar in a classroom.

College has another advantage—it gives you that much longer a time in which to grow. Once you get out in the world, you're faced with responsibilities you don't have in college. In college you have time to experiment, to fail, to think, to gain an understanding of who you are and what you want to do.

One alternative to college is the acting academy. Most academies operate on a two-year basis and only invite back for the second year students who have done well the first year. The obvious advantage of an acting academy over college is that everything you do is focused directly on the theater and on acting, whereas in a regular college you're involved in work and activities unrelated to drama. But the two—college and an acting academy—are not necessarily mutually exclusive. Many young people attend a regular four-year college, get a degree, and then enroll in an acting academy.

If you decide you don't want to go to college *or* an acting academy, there are still other approaches. Some people go to New York or Hollywood, get a job somewhere, perhaps waiting on table, and take acting lessons privately. I think it's difficult to break into the business this way, but it might work for you.

One thing I wouldn't advise is to go directly from high school to New York or Hollywood with the idea that you're going to start making the rounds and support yourself in the beginning by *acting* alone. You're far better off, I think, if you're just starting out, to try and get a job with a repertory company in another city. Get your experience there—two seasons at the minimum. Then you can think about going to New York. A number of successful actors broke into the business via the repertory companies outside of New York, among them Jane Alexander and George Grizzard.

If you decide to go to New York, regardless of where you've studied, you must go *prepared*. New York is an expensive city. The rents are very high, and just to get settled with an apartment and a phone will run to ~~hundreds~~ thousands of dollars.

You have to prepare yourself emotionally and psychologically as well. The pace and pressure of daily living in New York is far different from that in most cities. If you don't know anyone in New York, it can be an almost unbearably lonely place. I was fortunate in the beginning of my career. Since I was studying at Yale,

I had friends there and made other friends as soon as I started working in New York.

It helps to know someone already living in the city before you go: another actor, a friend from school—anybody who can help you make the difficult transition to New York living.

Probably the most discouraging time for any actor is the initial breaking in period. It doesn't dawn on most actors how overcrowded and competitive the business is until they start making the rounds, going to auditions, and knocking on the doors of producers and casting agents. You discover that there are actors who have been living and working in New York for as many as ten years and are still knocking on doors, still looking for a break of some kind. You find that actors you've seen in movies and on television are out of work, and you think, If *they're* having trouble finding work, where does this leave me? It's easy to get discouraged, and difficult to keep your faith and resolve.

One mistake actors frequently make when they first go to New York is to worry unnecessarily about getting an agent. An agent is someone who works for an actor in the following ways: he (or she) seeks out employment, negotiates contracts, and offers career guidance. Agents do not receive salaries or fees. They work on a strict commission basis—a percentage of an actor's earnings. An agent *per se* isn't going to get you work. He can arrange interviews and send you on auditions, but it's still up to you to impress the people doing the casting. If a director or producer thinks you can do a role, it doesn't matter whether you have an agent or not.

If you do have an agent, a good one can be an important asset. Ideally, you want someone who is concerned with you as a person and as an artist, somebody who will make decisions on the basis of what's good for you and your career. But not every agent falls into this category. Not all agents work for their actors equally hard.

Not having an agent doesn't mean you're *not* going to find work, and having one doesn't mean that you're going to find work. Much of the job-seeking an agent does, you can do on your own by keeping up with the casting notices published in the weekly trade journals, such as *Variety*, *Show Business*, and *Back Stage*.

One prominent agent in New York gives this advice to the young actor: "Few good agents will take on a new actor unless they've seen the actor's work. I always tell actors who come to see us: Get a role first. Anywhere. You'll find a job somewhere. Everybody does. Then contact us and we'll come down and watch you perform. If we think we can get work for you, we'll sit down and talk with you."

Something else you shouldn't worry about in the beginning of your career is becoming a member of Actors Equity, or the Screen Actors Guild, the trade union of television and movie actors. The best way to become a member of either of these unions is to first get a job in a company that is governed by Equity or the Screen Actors Guild. Equity used to have an apprentice program, but the decline of summer stock jobs has cut down the number of opportunities. Remember, though, a producer can hire anybody he wants. In other words, you don't have to be a member of Equity to get a job. Once you've become a member of an Equity cast, however, you do have to join the union.

Many non-Equity companies operate in New York and in other cities. They pay very little and the working conditions aren't always the most ideal, but it's still work and often valuable experience, and a chance to be seen. The worst thing for an actor is inactivity. As long as you're working on a role, it doesn't really matter where you're working.

Acting in television commercials has come into its own in recent years, creating new opportunities for actors, possibly the most lucrative opportunities in the acting business today. Here again, an agent can be helpful but is not essential. Some larger advertising agencies have their own casting directors and testing studios. They hold their own auditions. The trouble is, so many opportunities for commercial parts come up so quickly, it's difficult to keep track of what's going on—here's where an agent can be helpful.

At one time there was a stigma attached to working in a television commercial, but nowadays so many prominent actors do it, or have done it, it has become an accepted part of the profession. Certain actors still refuse to appear on-camera, agreeing only to supply narration, which is known as "voice-over" work, but most young actors actively look for work in TV commericals. The money is good; and there's always the chance that it might lead to something else.

One nice thing about television commercials is that a person with unusual looks often gets a chance he wouldn't normally get in a movie or a television series. Many agencies are getting away from leading-man and leading-lady types, and this has opened up a big field for character actors. Still, work in commercials is every bit as competitive—perhaps more so—than regular work in the theater, and it can be every bit as discouraging.

A few other things are worth mentioning. First, photographs. You don't have to spend a lot of money in the beginning. One good eight-by-ten portrait is all you generally need, along with a detailed résumé of all the parts you've done, in college or anywhere else. An average photographer will charge $25 a sitting and $5 for each eight-by-ten print. You can take that print to a reproduction studio and make dozens of reproductions at a modest price. You will need enough copies and résumés to leave one set with each producer you see. The big exception is for television commercials, where a portfolio of several photographs can be helpful. But this can also be expensive. Before you go looking for a photographer, speak with other actors.

Above all, be wary of talent agents and managers who want to sign you to contracts without having seen your work. Indeed, beware of anyone who promises instant success. There are no shortcuts to acting success, and anyone who tells you differently is creating a false picture.

Remember, too, that no one is going to come looking for you. Certainly, producers, agents, and directors are always looking for new talent, but you yourself have to go more than halfway. You have to keep at it. Interview after interview. Audition after audition. You can't allow yourself to be discouraged by a few unsuccessful auditions. You can't just sit by the phone and wait for an agent to call you. You must do most of the groundwork on your own. Once you've become established, then you can sit back and let an agent go out and find the work. In the beginning, it's up to you, to your desire, your energy, your determination, and your belief in yourself.

If I were asked to choose the most important quality a young actor needs, I would say without hesitation, courage. Everything else that it takes to make a fine actor—the tools, the motivation, and yes, the luck—none of it will mean anything if you don't have the courage to keep plugging away when prospects are their dimmest.

You *will* be disappointed. You *will* be discouraged. You *will* go through periods of doubt and depression. You *will* be tempted to quit. But if you are strong enough and determined enough and if you work hard enough to develop your talent, you have a good chance of making it.

The novelist William Faulkner was once asked what he thought to be the secret of success in life.

"Endure!" he said.

·16·

FINAL WORDS

Success is counted sweetest
By those who ne'er succeed.

—EMILY DICKINSON

In the preceding chapters I have tried to emphasize that acting is a unique profession. I won't say it is any better or any worse than other kinds of work, only that it is different. It is more than a craft, more than an art form, more than a way of earning a living. It is, as many actors have said many times, a way of life. And a very demanding way of life.

The demands come not from just the work itself. If you want to act, you must be prepared to make a great many sacrifices. It's important that you understand these sacrifices now and that you go into acting knowing full well you'll have to make them.

If your purpose in life, for instance, is solely to make a lot of money in a hurry, you should not go into acting. True, some actors make enormous salaries, but even the richest of them usually have experienced many lean years first. The fact is, most actors in America do not make enough money to support a family.

You must also have patience—a great deal of patience. It has been said before, but it bears repeating here. Many actors have worked for years and years before becoming successes overnight. If career success is your immediate and only goal, you probably won't take the time to really learn your craft. You won't develop the skills and knowledge needed not only to *become* successful but to *remain* successful. Many actors have had good breaks early in their careers but have lacked the discipline and the talent to solidify their early success. They soon faded from the public mind.

Success—especially early success—can be an actor's worst enemy. It can stunt your artistic growth. Once you've reached a certain level in your career, you're likely to become less adventurous in your choice of roles. Failure will haunt you more than ever before. You may play it safe, stop studying, and stagnate as a artist. Stanislavski warned: Once you stop studying, your growth and creativity come to an end.

As an actor, you'll have to make many sacrifices in your personal life. Acting isn't for you if what you want from life is to live "normally"—to settle down somewhere with a wife or a husband and have a family. I won't say it is impossible for an actor to enjoy a full and rewarding family life. Some actors and actresses do. But even under normal circumstances marriage is challenging.

It is not difficult to understand why so many marriages involving actors end in divorce. Consider the fierce commitment an actor must bring to his work, the hours spent in study, the hours spent in performance and in travel, compounded by the circumstance of always meeting and becoming involved with new people. I've been married and divorced twice. It's difficult to say if either marriage would have worked out had I not been an actress, but I can't imagine how my being an actress was of any help.

It's easier, I think, for a man to act and be married than a woman. Most men have careers totally separate from their home life. For a woman, especially a woman with children, the separation is difficult. Acting has unique demands. Motherhood has unique demands. It's impossible to serve both to the fullest extent. Most actresses with children compromise in some way by trying to fill both roles, knowing that each will suffer. I have faced this dilemma myself. My son Peter was born in 1955. In the beginning, when he was an infant, it was easy to include him in my life. I simply took him with me whenever I toured. But as he grew older and into a life of his own, I became more and more aware of the conflict. It isn't something you ever resolve; it's something you learn to live with.

Actors, of course, are not alone in this dilemma. Any artist who marries and assumes obligations beyond those of his art faces the same conflict. The Russian ballet genius Nijinsky went mad, I believe, because he simply couldn't resolve the responsibility he felt for his family and the love and dedication he felt toward his art.

The hard truth is there is no way in the world that you can be true to both responsibilities. If you are going to commit yourself *entirely* to your work, then there is little room in your life for a family in the usual sense of the word. At the same time, if you are intent on having a family and living a "normal" life, you will be limiting your growth as an artist and your chances for success. There is no right or wrong. It is all a matter of personal goals and ambition.

As much as acting means to me personally and as much as I have given of myself to the theater, there are times when I wonder if I might not be happier today with a houseful of children. Then again, I think most people, no matter what they do, wonder at times if they've chosen the right field or might not be happier doing something else.

The important thing, though, isn't so much what you do but how you go about it. There are so many ways to live a full and rich life. Acting is only one of them. It has worked for me, and for many other actors. It could work for you.

So if you decide that you are going to become an actor, don't be afraid to seek the impossible. Acting, to me, has always seemed like something of a quest. The possibilities are endless. Some actors, once they've mastered their craft, become directors or producers—even writers. Some organize their own theatrical or film companies.

But none of this can happen unless you begin with a vision of who you are and what you're trying to do. Believe in yourself. You may disagree with everything I've said in this book, but if you disagree with conviction, I say, fine, break all the rules, do what *you* think is right.

El Cordobés, the legendary Spanish bullfighter, was once asked by an interviewer if a person could ever learn to become a great bullfighter. "There is no university for courage," El Cordobés answered.

And I would say the same about acting. Whatever

you learn in school or from acting lessons, whatever you learn from other actors—these can take you only so far: the rest must come from within yourself.

Don't lose faith in yourself. Don't be afraid of failure. A young actor asked me not long ago if I thought he was good enough to take a particular part he'd been offered. He wasn't sure he was "ready."

"You're never ready," I told him. "And you're never not ready. You *do* it. And even if you don't measure up, you still learn something from it." If I had waited until I thought I was "ready" for a big part, I would never have done *The Member of the Wedding* when I did.

As long as you have the taste for acting, the love for it, the courage to stick with it under the worst circumstances, when your illusions about the theater begin to crumble, when you discover meanness and pettiness in actors and actresses whom you've idolized, when none of the things you imagined about life in the theater turn out to be true—no matter what, continue to go at your work with love, with honesty, and with courage. The rest will take care of itself.

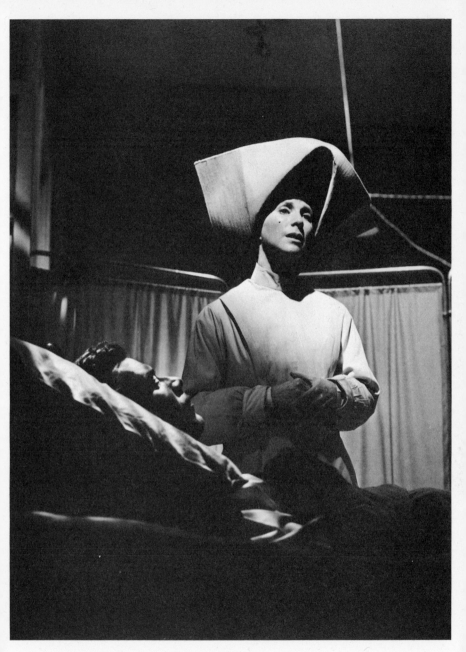

With Dirk Bogarde in *Little Moon of Alban*

With John Cecil Holm in *Forty Carats*. Photo by Friedman-Abeles

As Georgina in *Skyscraper*. United Press International Photo

With James Donald and John Williams in *Victoria Regina*

As Josefa in *A Shot in the Dark*. United Press
International Photo

As Victoria in *Victoria Regina* (TV).
United Press International Photo

As the Mexican girl in *The Power and the Glory* (TV).
United Press International Photo

With Steven Hill in *Sundown Beach*. Photo by Fred Fehl

As Sally Bowles in *I Am a Camera*

With Ethel Waters in *The Member of the Wedding*

As Liza Doolittle in *Pygmalion* (TV)

As June in *Marathon '33*

Recording a number from *Skyscraper*. United Press International Photo

As Joan in *The Lark*

Receiving the Tony Award for *Forty Carats*, with other 1969 winners: James Earl Jones, Angela Lansbury, and Jerry Orbach. United Press International Photo

With James Dean in *East of Eden* (film)

With James Dean in *East of Eden* (film)

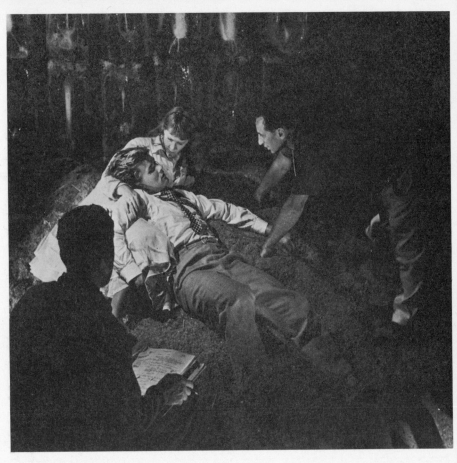

With Elia Kazan (right), filming a scene from *East of Eden*

With Staats Cotsworth in *Hamlet*. Photo by Keith B. Staulcup

As Sally Bowles in *I Am a Camera* (film)

With Laurence Harvey in *I Am a Camera* (film)

With Brandon de Wilde and Ethel Waters in *The Member of the Wedding* (film). Columbia Pictures Corp. Photo

With Boris Karloff in *The Lark* (TV)

With Laurence Harvey in *The Truth about Women* (film)

Reading from Emily Dickinson

JULIE HARRIS ON BROADWAY
Dates indicate opening night

Atlanta, in *It's a Gift*, by Curt Goetz. March 12, 1945.

Walk-on, in *Henry IV, Part II*, by William Shakespeare (Old Vic Company). May 13, 1946.

Walk-on, in *Oedipus*, by Sophocles (Old Vic Company). May 20, 1946.

Nelly, in *The Playboy of the Western World*, by J. M. Synge. October 26, 1946.

The White Rabbit (also understudy to Alice), in *Alice in Wonderland*, adapted from Lewis Carroll. May 28, 1947.

Third Witch, in *Macbeth*, by William Shakespeare (National Theatre Company). March 31, 1948.

Ida Mae, in *Sundown Beach*, by Bessie Breuer (Actors Studio Production). September 7, 1948.

Nancy Gear, in *The Young and the Fair*, by N. Richard Nash. November 22, 1948.

Angel Tuttle, in *Magnolia Alley*, by George Batson. April 18, 1949.

Felisa, in *Montserrat*, adapted by Lillian Hellman. October 29, 1949.

Frankie Addams, in *The Member of the Wedding*, by Carson McCullers. January 5, 1950.

Sally Bowles, in *I Am a Camera*, by John van Druten, based on stories by Christopher Isherwood. November 28, 1951.

Colombe, in *Mademoiselle Colombe*, by Jean Anouilh. January 6, 1954.

Joan, in *The Lark*, by Jean Anouilh. November 17, 1955.

Margery Pinchwife, in *The Country Wife*, by William Wycherly. November 27, 1957.

Ruth Arnold, in *The Warm Peninsula*, by Joe Masterhoff. October 29, 1959.

Brigid Mary, in *Little Moon of Alban*, by James Costigan. December 1, 1960.

Josefa, in *A Shot in the Dark*, by Marcel Achard, adapted by Harry Kurnitz. October 18, 1961.

June, in *Marathon '33*, by June Havoc. December 27, 1963.

Annie, in *Ready When You Are, C.B.*, by Susan Slade. December 7, 1964.

Georgina, in *Skyscraper*, musical based on Elmer Rice's *Dream Girl*. November 13, 1965.

Ann Stanley, in *Forty Carats*, adapted by Jay Allen. December 26, 1968.

Anna Reardon, in *And Miss Reardon Drinks a Little*, by Paul Zindel. February 25, 1971.

JULIE HARRIS OFF BROADWAY

The Glass Menagerie, by Tennessee Williams
The Hostage, by Brendan Behan
King John, by William Shakespeare
The Little Foxes, by Lillian Hellman
Peg of My Heart, by J. Hartley Manners
The Philadelphia Story, by Phillip Barry
Romeo and Juliet, by William Shakespeare
A Streetcar Named Desire, by Tennessee Williams
The Women, by Clare Boothe Luce

JULIE HARRIS MOVIES

East of Eden
Harper
The Haunting
I Am a Camera
The Member of the Wedding
The People Next Door
The Poacher's Daughter
Reflections in a Golden Eye
Requiem for a Heavyweight
The Split
The Truth About Women
You're a Big Boy Now

JULIE HARRIS ON TELEVISION

Anastasia
The Big Valley
Bonanza
A Doll's House
Ethan Frome
Garrison's Gorillas
The Good Fairy
He Who Gets Slapped
The Heiress
The Holy Terror

How Awful About Allan
Johnny Belinda
The Lark
Little Moon of Alban
The Night of the Storm
The Power and the Glory
Pygmalion
Rawhide
Turn the Key Deftly
Victoria Regina
A Wind From the South
Also, guest appearances in *Tarzan, The Name of the Game, Run for Your Life, Laredo,* and *The Men From Shiloh*

COLLEGES AND UNIVERSITIES
THAT OFFER DEGREE PROGRAMS
IN THEATER ARTS AND DRAMA

Nearly every college in the United States has some sort of theatrical program, either an on-campus theater group or an academic program in the theater arts. In some schools, acting courses are offered as part of a Speech Department's curriculum. In other schools, the Theater Department is a unit unto itself. The following list is based on information compiled in the Directory of American College Theatres, published in 1967 at Southern Methodist University. The schools listed are those that offer a minimum of twenty courses in the theater arts and related fields or have a theater group that has achieved distinction. Details such as admission requirements, scholarship aid, and specific courses offered can be found in the catalog of each school. To obtain a copy of a school catalog, address your request to the Drama Department.

English theater schools—The Royal Academy and others—also accept American students. Auditions are held twice a year.

Antioch College
Yellow Springs, Ohio 45387

Baylor University
Waco, Tex. 76703

Boston University
147 Bay State Road
Boston, Mass. 02215

Bowling Green State University
Bowling Green, Ohio 43402

Brandeis University
Waltham, Mass. 02154

California State College at Fullerton
800 North State College Boulevard
Fullerton, Calif. 92631

California State College at Long Beach
6101 East Seventh Street
Long Beach, Calif. 90801

Carnegie-Mellon University
5000 Forbes Avenue
Pittsburgh, Pa. 15213

Central Washington State College
Ellensburg, Wash. 98926

Drake University
Des Moines, Iowa 50311

Eastern Michigan University
Ypsilanti, Mich. 48197

Florida State University
Tallahassee, Fla. 32306

Fresno State College
Fresno, Calif. 93726

Goodman Memorial Theatre and School of Drama
Chicago, Ill. 60603

Howard University
Washington, D.C. 20001

Illinois State University
Normal, Ill. 61761

Illinois Wesleyan University
Bloomington, Ill. 61701

Kent State University
Kent, Ohio 44240

Los Angeles City College
855 North Vermont Avenue
Los Angeles, Calif. 90029

Los Angeles Valley College
5800 Fulton Avenue
Van Nuys, Calif. 91401

Louisiana State University in
New Orleans
Lakefront
New Orleans, La. 70122

Michigan State University
East Lansing, Mich. 48823

New York University
Washington Square
New York, N.Y. 10003

Northeastern University
360 Huntington Avenue
Boston, Mass. 02115

Northwestern University
Evanston, Ill. 60201

Ohio State University
Columbus, Ohio 43210

Ohio University
Athens, Ohio 45701

Pasadena Playhouse College
of Theatre Arts
39 South El Molino Avenue
Pasadena, Calif. 91101

Purdue University
West Lafayette, Ind. 47907

Queens College of the City
University of New York
65-30 Kissena Boulevard
Flushing, N.Y. 11367

Sacramento State College
6000 J Street
Sacramento, Calif. 95819

San Francisco State College
San Francisco, Calif. 94132

San Jose State College
San Jose, Calif. 95114

Sarah Lawrence College
Bronxville, N.Y. 10708

Southern Illinois University
Carbondale, Ill. 62903

Southern Methodist University
Dallas, Tex. 75222

Southern Oregon College
Ashland, Ore. 97520

Syracuse University
Syracuse, N.Y. 13210

Tufts College of Tufts University
Medford, Mass. 02155

United States International University
San Diego, Calif. 92101

University of Arizona
Park Avenue at East Third Street
Tucson, Ariz. 85721

University of California at Berkeley
Berkeley, Calif. 94720

University of California at Irvine
Irvine, Calif. 92664

University of California at Los Angeles
Los Angeles, Calif. 90024

University of California at Santa Barbara
Santa Barbara, Calif. 93106

University of Colorado
Boulder, Colo. 80302

University of Connecticut
Storrs, Conn. 06268

University of Denver
University Park
Denver, Colo. 80210

University of Georgia
Athens, Ga. 30601

University of Illinois
Urbana-Champaign Campus, Ill. 61803

University of Iowa
Iowa City, Iowa 52240

University of Miami
Coral Gables, Fla. 33124

University of Michigan
Ann Arbor, Mich. 48104

University of Minnesota
Minneapolis, Minn. 55455

University of Mississippi
University, Miss 38677

University of Montana
Missoula, Mont. 59801

University of New Mexico
Albuquerque, N.M. 87106

University of Oklahoma
Norman, Okla. 73069

University of Oregon
Eugene, Ore. 97403

University of South Dakota
Vermillion, S.D. 57069

University of Southern
  California
University Park
Los Angeles, Calif. 90007

University of Southern
  Mississippi
Hattiesburg, Miss. 39401

University of Texas at Austin
Austin, Tex. 78712

University of Utah
Salt Lake City, Utah 84112

University of Wisconsin
Madison, Wis. 53706

University of Wisconsin-
  Milwaukee
3203 North Downer Avenue
Milwaukee, Wis. 53201

Virginia Commonwealth
  University
901 West Franklin Street
Richmond, Va. 23220

Washington University
St. Louis, Mo. 63130

Wayne State University
Detroit, Mich. 48202

Weber State College
3750 Harrison Boulevard
Ogden, Utah 84403

Western Carolina University
Cullowhee, N.C. 28723

Yale University
New Haven, Conn. 06520

Leading Acting Schools and Academies in New York City (Write for catalog and details.)

Actors Studio
432 West 44th Street
New York, N.Y. 10036

American Academy of Dramatic Arts
120 Madison Avenue
New York, N.Y. 10016

American Musical and Dramatic Academy
150 Bleecker Street
New York, N. Y. 10012

Drama Division, Julliard School
Lincoln Center Plaza
New York, N.Y. 10023

Herbert Berghof Studio (also called HB Studio)
120 Bank Street
New York, N.Y. 10014

Neighborhood Playhouse
340 East 54th Street
New York, N.Y. 10022

Stella Adler Theatrical Studio
1974 Broadway
New York, N.Y. 10019

FOR FURTHER READING

Barrymore, Ethel, *Memories: An Autobiography*. New York, Harper & Brothers, 1955.

Blunt, Jerry, *The Composite Art of Acting*. New York, Macmillan, 1966.

Chekhov, Michael, *To the Actor*. New York, Harper & Row, 1953.

Cole, Toby, and Chinoy, Helen Krich, editors, *Actors on Acting*, rev. ed. New York, Crown, 1970.

Cornell, Katharine, *I Wanted to Be an Actress*, as told to Ruth Woodbury Sedgwood. New York, Random House, 1938.

Corson, Richard, *Stage Makeup*, 4th ed. New York, Hawthorn Books, 1967.

Craig, Edward G., *Ellen Terry and Her Secret Self*. New York, Benjamin Blom, 1932.

Eustis, Morton, *Players at Work*. New York, Theatre Arts, 1937.

Funke, Lewis, and Booth, John E., editors, *Actors Talk about Acting*. New York, Random House, 1961.

Garrick, David. Several biographies and collections of letters.

Gielgud, John, *Early Stages*. New York, Macmillan, 1939.

Gish, Lillian, *The Movies, Mr. Griffith & Me*, with Ann Pinchot. New York, Prentice-Hall, 1969.

Goldman, William, *The Season: A Candid Look at Broadway*. New York, Harcourt, Brace Javanovich, 1969.

Grotowski, Jerzy, *Towards a Poor Theatre*. New York, Simon and Schuster, 1970.

Gruen, John, *Close-Up*. New York, Viking, 1968.

Guthrie, Tyrone, *A Life in the Theatre*. New York, McGraw-Hill, 1959.

Hart, Moss, *Act One*. New York, Random House, 1959.

Hayes, Helen, *On Reflection: An Autiobiography*, with Sanford Dody. New York, M. Evans, 1968.

Hodapp, William, *The Television Actors' Manual*. New York, Appleton-Century-Crofts, 1955.

Maxwell, Gilbert, *Tennessee Williams and Friends*. New York, World, 1965.

Moore, Sonia, *The Stanislavski System*. New York, Viking, 1965.

Nyquist, Roy, *Showcase*. New York, William Morrow, 1966.

Perrotet, Phillipe, *Practical Stage Makeup*. New York, Van Nostrand Reinhold, 1967.

Redfield, William, *Letters from an Actor*. New York, Viking, 1967.

Rheinhardt, Emil A., *Life of Eleanora Duse*. New York, Benjamin Blom, 1930.

Reed, Rex, *Conversations in the Raw*. New York, World, 1969. *Do You Sleep in the Nude?* New York, New American Library, 1968.

Skinner, Cornelia Otis, *Madame Sarah*. Boston, Houghton Mifflin, 1967.

Stanislavski, Constantin, all works, particularly *An Actor Prepares*, translated by Elizabeth Reynolds Hapgood. New York, Theatre Arts, 1948.

Strasberg, Lee, *Strasberg at the Actors Studio*. New York, Viking, 1965.

Terry, Ellen, *Ellen Terry's Memoirs*, edited by Edith Craig and Christopher St. John. New York, Benjamin Blom.

Tairov, Alexander, *Notes of a Director*, edited by H. D. Albright, translated by William Kuhlke. Coral Gables, Fla., University of Miami Press, 1969.

Winter, William, *Life and Art of Edwin Booth*. Westport, Conn., Greenwood Press, 1968.

INDEX

d/A   Av/ac
    act/act.